CRITICAL
THE WORKS

MU00775550

The Last to Fall

"Authors Jim Rada and Richard Fulton have done an outstanding job of researching and chronicling this little-known story of those Marines in 1922, marking it as a significant moment in Marine Corps history."

- *GySgt. Thomas Williams*
Executive Director
U.S. Marine Corps Historical Company

"Original, unique, profusely illustrated throughout, exceptionally well researched, informed, informative, and a bit iconoclastic, "The Last to Fall: The 1922 March, Battles, & Deaths of U.S. Marines at Gettysburg" will prove to be of enormous interest to military buffs and historians."

- *Small Press Bookwatch*

Saving Shallmar

"But Saving Shallmar's Christmas story is a tale of compassion and charity, and the will to help fellow human beings not only survive, but also be ready to spring into action when a new opportunity presents itself. Bittersweet yet heartwarming, Saving Shallmar is a wonderful Christmas season story for readers of all ages and backgrounds, highly recommended."

- *Small Press Bookwatch*

Battlefield Angels

"Rada describes women religious who selflessly performed life-saving work in often miserable conditions and thereby gained the admiration and respect of countless contemporaries. In so doing, Rada offers an appealing narrative and an entry point into the wealth of sources kept by the sisters."

- *Catholic News Service*

Between Rail and River

"The book is an enjoyable, clean family read, with characters young and old for a broad-based appeal to both teens and adults. Between Rail and River also provides a unique, regional appeal, as it teaches about a particular group of people, ordinary working 'canawlers' in a story that goes beyond the usual coverage of life during the Civil War."

- *Historical Fiction Review*

Canawlers

"A powerful, thoughtful and fascinating historical novel, Canawlers documents author James Rada, Jr. as a writer of considerable and deftly expressed storytelling talent."

- *Midwest Book Review*

"James Rada, of Cumberland, has written a historical novel for high-schoolers and adults, which relates the adventures, hardships and ultimate tragedy of a family of boaters on the C&O Canal. … The tale moves quickly and should hold the attention of readers looking for an imaginative adventure set on the canal at a critical time in history."

- *Along the Towpath*

October Mourning

"This is a very good, and very easy to read, novel about a famous, yet unknown, bit of 20th Century American history. While reading this book, in your mind, replace all mentions of 'Spanish Flu' with 'bird flu.' Hmmm."

- *Reviewer's Bookwatch*

SECRETS OF
CATOCTIN MOUNTAIN

Little-Known Stories & Hidden History
Along Catoctin Mountain

Other books by James Rada, Jr.

Non-Fiction
- Battlefield Angels: The Daughters of Charity Work as Civil War Nurses
- Beyond the Battlefield: Stories from Gettysburg's Rich History
- Clay Soldiers: One Marine's Story of War, Art, & Atomic Energy
- Echoes of War Drums: The Civil War in Mountain Maryland
- The Last to Fall: The 1922 March, Battles & Deaths of U.S. Marines at Gettysburg
- Looking Back: True Stories of Mountain Maryland
- Looking Back II: More True Stories of Mountain Maryland
- No North, No South: The Grand Reunion at the 50th Anniversary of the Battle of Gettysburg
- Saving Shallmar: Christmas Spirit in a Coal Town

Other Books in the Secrets Series
- Secrets of Garrett County: Little-Known Stories & Hidden History of Maryland's Westernmost County

Fiction
- Between Rail and River
- Canawlers
- Lock Ready
- October Mourning
- The Rain Man

SECRETS OF
CATOCTIN MOUNTAIN

Little-Known Stories & Hidden History
Along Catoctin Mountain

by
James Rada, Jr.

LEGACY
PUBLISHING

A division of AIM Publishing Group

SECRETS OF CATOCTIN MOUNTAIN: LITTLE-KNOWN STORIES
AND HIDDEN HISTORY ALONG CATOCTIN MOUNTAIN

Published by Legacy Publishing, a division of AIM Publishing Group.
Gettysburg, Pennsylvania.
Copyright © 2017 by James Rada, Jr.
All rights reserved.
Printed in the United States of America.
First printing: June 2017.

ISBN 978-0-9985542-5-9

This is a collection primarily of articles that have previously appeared in
The Catoctin Banner, Maryland Life, Frederick, The Thurmont Dispatch,
and *The Emmitsburg Dispatch*. In some cases where additional information is available the stories have been updated.

Cover design by Grace Eyler.

LEGACY
PUBLISHING

315 Oak Lane • Gettysburg, Pennsylvania 17325

To John Kinnaird,
a friend who loves the Catoctin Mountain Area and
is generous with his knowledge, materials, and pictures.

CONTENTS

Where is Catoctin Mountain?

C atoctin Mountain is a single mountain ridge that runs through Frederick County, Maryland, into Loudoun County, Virginia. So it's not the Catoctin Mountains, it is only Catoctin Mountain. It rises to 1,900 feet around Cunningham State Falls. In Frederick County, Catoctin Mountain runs parallel and close to South Mountain to the west.

The name Catoctin is believed to be derived from Kittocton, which was an American Indian tribe that lived at the foot of the mountain where it runs into the Potomac River. Local lore says that Catoctin means "place of many deer" in the Indian language.

Despite the fact that the name tongue ties some people (It's pronounced *Ka-Tock-Tin.*), it's an interesting word as are its people and stories.

However, there was a time before even the dinosaurs lived that Catoctin Mountain did not exist. Two-hundred-and-seventy-million years ago, give or take a few million years, the ever-so-slow collision of the earth's plates along the present-day East Coast caused the ground to buckle and fold in on itself and rise into the sky.

Around 220 million years ago, Frederick County (and, in fact, all of central Maryland) was part of a vast lake and mud flat that stretched from North Carolina to Connecticut. Catoctin Mountain was not the mere hills they are today, but an enormous range towering as high as the Himalayas. The lake, known as the Lockatong, sat in the middle of Pangaea, an immense, C-shaped supercontinent.

"These mountains were once as tall and jagged as the Rockies, but as the continents moved apart again, the pressure that had raised them eased," John Bedell, Gregory Katz, Jason Shellenhamer, Lisa Kraus, and Sarah Groesbeck wrote in *The People of the Mountain* for the National Park Service.

Because of Pangaea's massive size, most of the inland areas were arid. Lake Lockatong was one of the exceptions, though it could be more mud than water at times. Pangaea eventually broke apart, and the pieces would spread to become the continents we know today.

Lake Lockatong began to dry and, as it did, some of its fish and other creatures found themselves trapped in small pools of water. When those pools evaporated, the critters died in the mud. Their fossils have been discovered on farms in the area in recent years.

Small animals moved across the mud flats seeking water. Behind them, their prints remained, baked into permanence by the heat of the sun.

Years passed. Eons elapsed. The land changed. It cooled. Different types of vegetation arose. The mountains shrank due to eons of erosion. Man appeared.

And that is where our story begins.

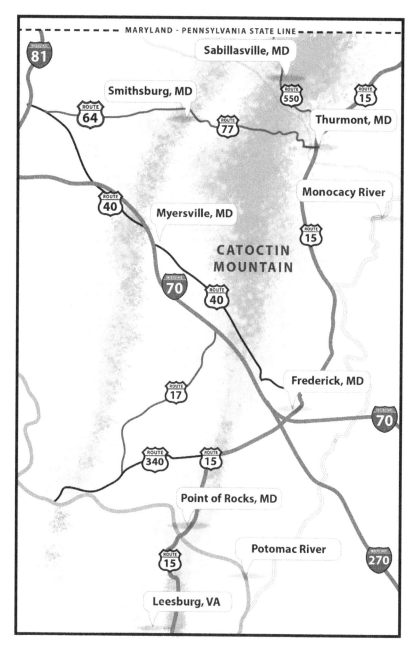

Catoctin Mountain runs from just north of Thurmont, Md., to just north of Leesburg, Va.

MOUNTAIN FOLK

The Zimmerman Family and Their Flying Machines

M an has long wanted to fly like the birds. Icarus and wings from Greek mythology are one of the early examples of this. The problem was that even as man learned how to leave the earth behind, he couldn't find a way to control his flight. He was at the mercy of the winds, much like the old sailing ships.

Then the Wright Brothers made the first controlled and sustained flight on a powered, heavier-than-air craft on December 17, 1903. The world changed.

One of the Wright Brothers' contemporaries was Dr. Charles Zimmerman of Braddock Heights, Md. He had been fascinated with flight for about as long as the Wrights had, and Anne Hooper in *Braddock Heights: a glance backwards* wrote that they Wrights and Zimmerman had corresponded.

Born in Charlestown, W.Va., in 1852, Zimmerman had moved to Frederick, Md., in 1893 after leaving his successful practice in New York because "it proved too onerous for his health," according to the *Frederick News*.

Soon after that, his experiments in creating a flying machine began. Small advertisements appeared in the newspapers offering a toy flying machines and tailless kites for 10 cents (about $5 in today's dollars).

These toys also served as the models for his own experiments in manned flight. In 1902, the newspaper began reporting that Zimmerman was close to creating an "aeroplane".

His goal was to have something that he could enter in the 1904 St. Louis World's Fair.

A volunteer glides through the air using one of the wings of Charles Zimmerman's flying machine.

A $100,000 prize (about $4.5 million in today's dollars) was being offered to the person who could navigate an airship over a 15-mile planned course in an hour. It was a sizable prize that attracted a lot of inventors.

By 1902, the Zimmermans were spending their summers in Braddock Heights where the doctor continued his experiments. It seemed that he was close and expected his flying machine to carry passengers. In an interview in the *Frederick News,* he said that he had made all of his friends and family parachutes "in case any should be timid enough to want to back out."

He noted that he had faced a lot of doubters, but he believed that man would be able to fly someday.

"We believe the aeroplane idea will come to the front and take the lead, soaring and flying over, under and around any balloon that was ever made, regardless of wind or weather, for the harder the wind blows the less work has the aeroplane man. He can go into the eye of the then, like an ice boat, or across or with the wind," Zimmerman told the newspaper.

The flying machine invented by Charles Zimmerman's sons gets a test flight.

The June 7, 1902, issue of the newspaper showed one of his experiments. One of the wings (which was 35 feet by 3 feet) of his craft was tethered to a tree and a seat attached to it. The picture showed the wind lifting a boy into the air.

Essentially, it was not much different than a parachute caught in an updraft.

Zimmerman's design called for two wings the size of the one on the picture.

"The operator grasps the inner end of wing arm with his hands, with his feet on the pedals on wheels, and flaps their wings up and down to get propulsion. The wheels enable the machine to run along on the ground until a speed of about 20 miles an hour is attained," *the Frederick News* reported.

The problem, admitted Zimmerman, was reaching the required 20 miles per hour. "I have not yet struck the happy combination of mechanical adjustment of parts of the machine to the highest ideal development of muscular energy of the human frame," he said.

The answer continued to elude him, and by September 1903, he had begun to doubt himself and the idea of flight, at least in the near future. He told a reporter that he questioned whether anyone would be able to win the $100,000 in St. Louis. It was just a few months later that the Wright Brothers made their historic flight, and Zimmerman's enthusiasm was rekindled.

He was correct about the World's Fair prize, though. No one captured the award in St. Louis the following year. However, Roy Knabenshue did pilot the "California Arrow," a powered balloon, on a 37-minute flight 2,000 feet above the fairgrounds. It was the most successful of several airships and balloons that tried for the prize.

T. S. Baldwin built the "California Arrow." From pictures, it resembles what would eventually become a dirigible. In fact, Knabenshue would go on to become the country's first dirigible pilot and build the first passenger dirigible in America. The "California Arrow" only carried one person, though. Knabenshue stood on a triangular frame below an oblong balloon. He turned the airship by shifting his weight to one side or the other.

Zimmerman's health soon deteriorated, and he died from tuberculosis on March 5, 1908, at the age of 56. He left behind a wife and four children. His sons, Charles and Harry, soon took up their father's passion with a goal of making his dream a reality as a way to honor their father.

On September 5, 1908, the Zimmerman Brothers demonstrated their own flying machine, which was based on their father's designs. They took the machine up on National Pike as it crossed the top of Catoctin Mountain and started down toward Middletown.

A young boy named Russell Lowe, who weighed 110 pounds, was strapped into the seat of the craft, which was pointed into the wind.

"The wind raised the machine from the ground, and sustained it while it was propelled a distance of about 25 feet, when it was pulled to the ground," the *Frederick News* reported.

The flight was repeated a few hours later with Robert McCutcheon as the pilot.

While the Zimmermans' airplane test was successful, the newspaper noted, "While the circular plane intended to maintain the equilibrium of the machine could not be revolved fast enough to demonstrate its worth, the inventors were much pleased with the demonstration of the sustaining power of the planes of the machine."

The flight must have ignited an interest in flying in McCutcheon. Hooper noted in her book that McCutcheon with the help of the Keller Brothers would go on to build a bi-plane glider that was able to fly.

How a Lincoln Conspirator
Came to Call Emmitsburg Home

J ohn Surratt Jr. hated life in Emmitsburg, Md., but then he hated life in America. Maybe that was why he tried to kidnap the President of the United States.

Surratt was born April 13, 1844, in Washington, D.C., the youngest of John and Mary Surratt's five children. When the Civil War broke out, Surratt was attending St. Charles College near Baltimore. His father died in 1862 while Surratt was home, and he did not return to complete his schooling. Instead, he was appointed U.S. Postmaster of Surrattsville, Md., but he also became a postmaster of sorts for the Confederacy. He carried letters and troop information to Confederate boats on the Potomac River.

"We had a regular established line from Washington to the Potomac, and I being the only unmarried man on the route, I had most of the hard riding to do. I devised various ways to carry the dispatches - sometimes in the heel of my boots, sometimes between the planks of the buggy," Surratt said in an 1870 speech.

Samuel Mudd introduced Surratt to John Wilkes Booth on December 23, 1864, in Washington. Surratt willingly joined in Booth's conspiracy to abduct President Abraham Lincoln by stopping his carriage while it was en route to a destination.

"To our great disappointment, however, the President was not there but one of the government officials - Mr.

[Salmon P.] Chase, if I mistake not. We did not disturb him, as we wanted a bigger chase than he could have afforded us. It was certainly a bitter disappointment, but yet I think a most fortunate one for us. It was our last attempt," Surratt said.

John Wilkes Booth assassinates President Abraham Lincoln at Ford's Theater. Photo courtesy of the Library of Congress.

On the night Booth and some of Surratt's other co-conspirators attempted a triple assassination of Lincoln, the vice president and the secretary of state, Surratt said he was in Elmira, N.Y., spying for the Confederacy. However, it was believed initially that Surratt attempted to assassinate the secretary of state. Surratt found himself a wanted man with a $25,000 bounty on his head.

Surratt fled to Canada. "A parish priest, Father Charles Boucher, gave sanctuary to the former Catholic seminarian, and Surratt remained there in hiding from mid-April through the trial, conviction, sentencing, and hanging of his mother. He followed the trial by reading the papers, and through secret correspondence with friends in Washington. In all that time, from the end of April to the first week of July, Surratt made no effort to save his mother from the gallows. Later, he blamed his friends for failing to inform him about the true peril that Mary Surratt faced," James Swanson wrote in *Manhunt: The 12-Day Chase for Lincoln's Killer.*

Mary Surratt was arrested tried and hanged with three other conspirators – George Atzerodt, Lewis Paine, and David Herold.

From Canada, Surratt fled to England in September 1865 and then onto Rome, where he joined the Papal Zouaves, the army of the Papal States. On a trip to Egypt in 1866, Surratt was identified as a Lincoln conspirator and arrested.

John Surratt's mother, Mary, was among the four conspirators tried and hanged for their roles in Lincoln's assassination. Photo courtesy of the Library of Congress.

One of the first wanted posters issued after the assassination lists a $25,000 reward for Surratt's capture as an accomplice of John Wilkes Booth. Photo courtesy of the Library of Congress.

He was returned to the United States where he stood trial in a civilian court that began on June 10, 1867. After testimony from 170 witnesses, the trial ended two months later with a hung jury. The government eventually dropped the charges and Surratt was freed in the summer of 1868.

"John Surratt was a free man. His mother was dead, he had been exposed as a leader in a plot to kidnap President Lincoln, and he had earned the reputation of a coward who had abandoned his mother to die. But at least he was alive. If he had been captured in 1865 and tried by military tribunal, he certainly would have been convicted, and would likely have been executed," Swanson wrote.

Surratt sought to turn his experiences into a career on the lecture circuit. He readily admitted a part in the kidnapping but denied involvement in the assassination. When his speaking tour was canceled because of public outrage, Surratt took up teaching. Following a stint as a teacher at a school in Rockville, Md., he used his Catholic connections to secure a position in Emmitsburg.

One source puts Surratt in Emmitsburg as early as 1870, teaching at St. Joseph's School, which was identified as being held in the old fire hall opposite St. Joseph's Church.

"He rattled his classes and resorted to physical punishment to maintain discipline. On older boys, some of them twenty or twenty-one, he used his fists. The younger boys John would beat with a paddle after he had stretched them over a special punishment desk which he had designed," according to a 1938 letter by Frederick Welty.

Sandra Walia with the Surratt House Museum's James O. Hall Research Center doubts this could have been Surratt because his students nicknamed the man in Welty's letter "Old Bear" and Surratt would have only been about 27 years old at the time, barely older than the oldest boys he taught.

Another account, which comes directly from Surratt, said he left his teaching position in Rockville in 1873 and took a job as principal at St. Vincent's Academy in Emmitsburg with 60 students. This was probably St. Vincent's Hall, which was built in 1857 as a combination school and literary and social center next to St. Joseph's Church. The Daughters of Charity took over the teaching there in 1878, so the 1873 date for Surratt's tenure would have been right.

John Surratt in his uniform as a Papal Zouave in Rome. Photo courtesy of the Library of Congress.

During his time there, Surratt wrote to Father Jolivet who had sheltered him in England when he had fled Canada after Lincoln's assassination. "My greatest desire, Father Jolivet is to leave this abominable country and go to Europe there to spend the balance of my days in peace and quiet," Surratt wrote.

At the time Surratt wrote the letter, he had been married 11 months to Mary Victorine Hunter, a second cousin of Francis Scott Key. He was also the father of a newborn son. Shortly after that, the Surratts moved to Baltimore where Surratt took a job at the Baltimore Steam Packet Company.

When he died of pneumonia on April 21, 1916, at age 72, he was the last surviving member of the Lincoln conspiracy and the only one known to have called Emmitsburg home.

Gentleman of the Old School

William McGill would have laughed at the idea that students need to be educated in $60-million-plus schools to get a good education. He would have known. For nearly a quarter-century, he taught school in the last one-room school in Frederick County.

"Some people are of the opinion that youngsters can't get an education in a one-room school. That isn't keeping with the facts," McGill told the *Sun Magazine* in 1952. "Since 1910, I've been teaching in schools like this, and I wish I had a dollar for every one of my pupils who went to the university. Why, last year Betty Ann Willard, a girl I taught, was the honor graduate at Thurmont High."

Philip's Delight

Philip's Delight School was located off an old lumber trail surrounded by thick woods high up on Catoctin Mountain. Before the school closed on February 1, 1955, the families on the mountain had had their own school since 1800.

Albert Hauver, a 96-year-old resident on the mountain, told McGill the history of the school in 1943. The families living on the mountain in 1800 sought a location to build a school for their children.

It is said that Philip Fox found a location and declared, "What a delightful spot for a building," according to McGill. People started calling the place Philip's Delight and built a log cabin on the site that served as the school until 1886. That year, the building burned down. Another building was constructed a short distance away that acted as the new school until 1932 when it also burned down. The final school building was brought into the area from Foxville, Md., and served until the school was closed. William Stump, writing for the *Sun Magazine*, said that the final building was "a dull, weather-beaten building, and the years have made it sway-backed, like an old plowhorse."

Students playing outside of the Phillips Delight School. Photo courtesy of Thurmontimages.com.

Despite its exterior, the school was relatively well equipped. McGill told *The Frederick News* in 1943, "Many visitors drop in on us during the school year and they frequently manifest surprise at our modern equipment, such as cards, charts, wall maps, textbooks, test materials and library books. The superintendent and supervisors have made it their policy to furnish all school children in the county with as near equal opportunities as possible."

During its 155 years, Philip's Delight was always a one-room school with never more than few dozen students in grades one through seven. When the school finally closed, it only had 13 students.

William McGill working with a group of younger students at his school. Photo courtesy of Thurmontimages.com.

William McGill

McGill was the last teacher at the school, and it was because of his strong support of the school that it remained open as long as it did.

When the school burned down in 1932, McGill told *The News*, "The superintendent's office said, 'Ah! Now we can bring those pupils down the hill to Thurmont.' So they announced that they were not going to rebuild, and they put on a new school bus. And you know what happened?

"It ran for four months, and it didn't have a single passenger!"

The families who lived on the mountain didn't want their children traveling on the narrow, winding road up and down the mountain twice a day. In the winter, the roads could quickly turn icy, which made them even more dangerous.

McGill volunteered to teach at the school, but after a few years was transferred to act as the principal at Foxville School. However, by 1946, the Philip's Delight School had gone through a number of teachers; none of whom wanted to teach in such a small school and isolated area. The Frederick County Board of Education began discussing closing the school, which parents again resisted vehemently.

McGill gave up his principalship and moved once again to Philip's Delight School where he taught until 1955.

McGill was the son of an Episcopal minister who was born near Catoctin Furnace. He attended Old St. Paul's School in Baltimore and Thurmont High, but he did not go to college initially. Once he was a teacher, he studied summers at Johns Hopkins and Western Maryland College.

He began teaching in Frederick County's small rural schools in 1910. He would instruct as many as 84 students at a time, some of them 21 years old.

"Got arrested twice for fighting with my pupils, then. They were as old as 21 in those days, and didn't have a whole lot of respect until I drilled it into them," McGill told *The News*.

Despite his early fights, McGill became a teacher who was loved and respected by his students and parents.

"He was the last of the one-room school teachers in the county, and in his early days he taught in areas where there were no communications and some of the patrons could not read or write. In some cases, Mr. McGill was the main liaison with the outside world for medical services, letter writing, and the like," *The News* reported.

In his later years, he was often called "Gentleman of the Old School."

During the 1940s, McGill would bike from Catoctin Furnace seven miles uphill along narrow roads to reach the school. If it were snowing, he would walk the distance. By the 1950's, McGill had added school bus driver (actually, it was a station wagon with "school bus" painted on the rear) to his duties, but this allowed him to be able to drive to school.

William McGill teaching students at the Phillips Delight School. Photo courtesy of Thurmontimages.com

School Days

During those last years of teaching at Philip's Delight, McGill's day began at 7 a.m. when he would get in the station wagon and drive up Catoctin Mountain on roads "so winding an narrow that he blows his horn constantly to warn the lumber wagons which frequently come the other way," Stump wrote. The change in elevation was 1,500 feet over six miles of road.

He would stop at the farms and cabins and pick up the older school children and then take them back down the mountain to Thurmont High School. Many of them were his former students so he would catch up with their lives and their studies during the trip.

Once he dropped them off, he would turn around and head back up the mountain. If he passed the homes of any of his current students, he would stop to pick them up. When they arrived at Philip's Delight School, it would already be warm because two students who lived closest to the school had the job each morning to fetch wood from the shed and get the fire started in the iron stove that served as the building's heating system.

"It was still cold at times because it wasn't insulated," said former student Austin Hurley of Thurmont.

Another former student, Betty Willard of Thurmont remembered that on those cold days the students were allowed to move their desks so that they were closer to the stove. Also, because the school did not have electricity when she attended, foggy days would make it hard to see inside the school since the windows were only on one side of the building. On those days, the students were allowed to move their desks closer to the windows in order to be able to read their books.

Like many other buildings on the mountain, Philip's Delight School had no indoor plumbing. The students had to use the two outhouses behind the school.

"You just had to watch out for snakes, bees, and spiders when you opened the door," Betty Willard said.

William McGill watches over his students at recess. Photo courtesy of Thurmontimages.com.

Inside the school, the wooden floor was black from the oil it was polished with to keep down the dust. Seven rows of desks filled the room and bookshelves, coat racks and blackboards were mounted on the walls. The walls needed a fresh coat of paint, but it was hard to tell this because posters covered just about all of the free space on the walls.

The posters were part of McGill's teaching style. He told *The News*, "If a fifth grader has forgotten something basic from the previous year all he has to do is look around. In fact, there's hardly a spot to rest a day-dreaming eye without absorbing knowledge."

Most of the student arrived by 8:30 a.m. The girls would often bring flowers to put in bottles to brighten the room. The boys would get buckets and walk down a lumber trail to the Willard Farm a quarter mile away. They would fill the buckets with water and then walk back to the school. The water they brought would be the school's water supply for the day.

The students each brought their own tin cup to school. If they got thirsty during the day, they would use a dipper to get water from a bucket and fill their cup.

The school had electricity, but only after January 1952. Up until that time, a student would ring a school bell to note the beginning of classes. After that time, an electric buzzer was used.

The school day started each morning with the students reciting The Lord's Prayer and the Pledge of Allegiance.

Then McGill would begin teaching his lessons to seven different grades of students with the skill of a master juggler. Stump described one scene this way:

"Seating the first-graders with picture books, he sends third, fourth and fifth graders to the blackboards with instructions to write the names of the characters in their books. Looking at his watch, he reads aloud with the seventh.

"McGill is not still for a second. Neither is he excited—although every second is one of enthusiasm for him," Stump wrote.

At lunchtime, many students walked home for lunch, but others ate at the school. Though some of the schools in Frederick got a hot lunch program earlier, hot meals didn't come to many of the county's rural schools until 1923 and even then, calling it a "hot lunch" was generous.

"At Philip's Delight hot cocoa is served at noon each day and the milk for this beverage is carried by the teacher for a distance of about six miles to the school. There are about 30 children enrolled in the school," *The News* reported.

Some other rural schools would have hot soup instead of cocoa. The purpose wasn't for the cocoa or soup to be lunch but to supplement the food the students brought from home.

Students gather firewood to heat the Phillips Delight one-room school. Photo courtesy of Thurmontimages.com

Before the students could eat their lunches, they would say grace. Then McGill would sit with them and talk while they ate.

After lunch, the student would play outside while McGill sat on the porch watching over them. Once recess had ended, there would be another session of afternoon classes until the day ended and McGill became a bus driver again.

Betty Willard remembered that McGill would also take the students on field trips. She recalled one such trip when McGill had all of the students bring a sack to take a field trip to gather mushrooms. However, as they walked through the woods to the mushrooms, McGill would have students identify trees and wildflowers that he pointed out.

McGill said of his teaching philosophy in *The News*, "I'm strong on fundamentals; you won't believe it, but I talked to a high-school student not long ago who said the capital of the United States was Annapolis. That why I stress places and locations so much; I've always done it and I always will.

"Yet it's more than that. I teach the fundamentals of religion—because there are no churches up here," McGill said in the *Sun Magazine*.

He put the school's location to his benefit in teaching, taking the students on walks in the woods to view animals or using acorns for counting. His goal was to keep them busy and to have fun and rarely did he have discipline problems.

"And in a school like this, every last pupil gets close attention from the teacher—and the young ones benefit from being in the same room with the older ones," he told *The News*.

Betty Willard enjoyed working with the younger students when she finished with her own lessons.

"I think that is where I got the desire to teach," Willard said. She taught school for 40 years, including teaching at the last two-room school in the county, which was in Foxville.

Closing the School

When McGill was transferred to Catoctin Furnace School in the middle of the 1954-1955 school year, no other teacher could be found to take his place at Philip's Delight and so the decision was made to close the school. With only 13 students in the school, Superintendent Eugene Pruitt decided that two-thirds of the costs to operate the school could be saved by bussing the students to Catoctin Furnace School, and as an added benefit, McGill would still be teaching them.

William McGill working with students. Photo courtesy of Thurmontimages.com.

McGill retired from teaching in 1958 at the mandatory age of 70.

"I've tried to give an education and make it pleasant for the pupils. I know I've had a good time," McGill told the *Frederick Post*.

When this teacher of the county's smallest schools died at age 85 in 1973, it made the front page in *The News*.

According to a former student, Gideon Willard of Thurmont, the school building sat deserted until 1961. After a snowstorm, the old roof was overburdened with snow and collapsed, and the school had to be torn down.

Though Philip's Delight was one of the last one-room schools in Maryland, the last one-room school to close down was in Tylerton, a small island community in the Chesapeake Bay. When it closed in 1994, it had only nine students with five of them moving on to middle school the next year.

William McGill teaching at Phillips Delight School. Photo courtesy of Thurmontimages.com.

The First American-Born Saint

E lizabeth Ann Seton was not a canonized saint when she first arrived in Emmitsburg, Md. She was the merely the mother of her own children and a new community of religious women sisters, the first native sisterhood established in the United States. She was hoping to teach young girls, especially those from poor families, and prepare them for the future, but in doing so, she left a legacy that is still felt today.

Seton arrived in Emmitsburg in June of 1809 to form a religious community for women with a mission of education and charity. She found not a city like New York or Baltimore, but a small town that wasn't 25 years old. Yet, what the town lacked in population, it made up for in faith; however, it was not the Catholic faith. Emmitsburg's predominant faiths were Presbyterian and Lutheran, though the Catholics had made their presence known with Sulpician priest John Dubois establishment of Mount St. Mary's, the second Catholic college and seminary in the country, in 1808.

The 50-mile journey from Baltimore had been uncomfortable with the women who walked beside their covered wagon in the sticky heat of a Maryland summer.

Elizabeth wrote of the trip, "The dogs and pigs came out to meet us, and the geese stretched their necks in mute demand to know if we were any of their company, to which we gave assent."

She was a tiny powerhouse of spiritual fervor, which would be needed to form a community of sisters. She was a small woman, slender and graceful. She had large, brown eyes, naturally curly hair and beautiful features set in an oval face that had made her sought after in her youth. She was a 34-year-old widow with five children and a newly appointed mother superior of a handful of sisters.

With Elizabeth were her oldest daughter Anna Maria, sisters-in-law Cecelia and Harriet Seton and Sister Maria Murphy. Dubois, President of Mount St. Mary's College, which had been founded the prior year, gave them the use of his two-room cottage until a more permanent home could be built to house them. He moved into the seminary to accommodate the sisters until they could move into the old Fleming farmhouse in St. Joseph's Valley.

Despite having lodgings, the women's first winter in the Emmitsburg area was a rough one. "As might be expected in the drafty little cottage - snow actually sifted into the garret and partially covered the sisters sleeping there - sickness was a commonplace that winter," Joseph Dirvin, C.M., wrote in *Mrs. Seton Foundress of the American Sisters of Charity.* Elizabeth's son William was sick enough that his death shroud was made for him by his Aunt Harriet but he recovered, and Harriet soon died unexpectedly.

The nearness of Mount St. Mary's College also gave the new sisterhood access to Sulpician priests who could assure the women of counsel, confessors, and daily Mass.

The new home for Elizabeth and her sisters was financed by a gift from Samuel Sutherland Cooper, a wealthy Catholic convert who had entered St. Mary's Seminary in Baltimore. He and the Sulpician priests, Dubois and Louis W. Dubourg, purchased a stone farmhouse and property from Robert Fleming for the women soon after the women arrived.

The story of how Cooper became Seton's benefactor is told by Dirvin, in his booklet, "Blessed Elizabeth Ann Seton":

Elizabeth Ann Seton

Beginnings

Seton was an unlikely mother superior in a small, country community, but life had shaped her through a variety of experiences to make her aptly suited for the challenges she faced.

She was born into New York society on August 28, 1774, and was baptized into the Episcopalian faith in New York. Her father, Richard Bayley, was a well-known doctor who became New York City's first public health officer. Her mother, Catherine Charlton Bayley, was the daughter of a devout Episcopalian minister.

Elizabeth married William Magee Seton on January 25, 1794. He was 25, and she was 19. Their marriage was a happy one into which their first daughter Anna Maria was born a year later. William was born in November 1796.

As a society matron, Elizabeth along with others was a founding member of the Widows' Society in 1797. The women visited widows in their homes providing social services and nursed and comforted them.

The Seton's third child, Richard Bayley, was born in July 1798.

In 1799, her husband's company failed, and the family lost everything, filing for bankruptcy in 1800.

A fourth child, Catherine Charlton, was born in 1800. In August 1802, the Seton's last child, Rebecca, was born.

William Seton, with his health failing, decided to visit business associates in Italy in the hopes that the sea voyage and change might improve his health.

Elizabeth and Anna Maria accompanied him while the rest of the children stayed with family in New York. The effort was too little, too late. Will died in Pisa on December 27, 1803, after having been in Italy a little over a month. Elizabeth kept a moving journal of this trial, and her experience in Italy which is published in *Elizabeth Bayley Seton Collected Writings*, vol. 1.

Following William's death, his business associates, Filippo and Antonio Filicchi and their wives, provided hospitality to Elizabeth and Anna Marie and began to teach Elizabeth about Catholicism. Delays kept Elizabeth and Anna Marie in Italy until 1804, and when she sailed home, Antonio accompanied them and continued explaining Catholic teachings.

When Elizabeth finally announced she was thinking of becoming a Catholic, she met shock and resistance in New York. Catholics at the time were looked down upon and discriminated against. Friends and family rushed to bring her back to the fold and for a time were successful.

However, in March of 1805, Elizabeth made her profession of faith in the Catholic Church. Becoming a Catholic did not make it any easier for her to earn a living. The Filicchis had been supporting her, but Elizabeth needed to find a way to make her own living.

Many of her friends in New York were shocked and very upset at her choice. Elizabeth met rejection and public humiliation for becoming a Catholic.

Ostracized, Elizabeth and her children left for Baltimore. Father William Valentine Dubourg, president of Saint Mary's College and Seminary in Baltimore, invited Elizabeth to start a school for girls in the city. In trying to encourage her to move to Baltimore, Father Francis Matignon of Boston told Elizabeth, "You are destined, I think, for some great good in the United States."

Elizabeth arrived in Baltimore on June 15, 1808, with her daughters. Her sons were already attending Georgetown College, having gained admittance there with the help of Antonio Filicchi and Bishop John Carroll.

Elizabeth's home on Paca Street also served as her first Catholic School. Besides her and her three daughters, it housed four boarding students.

The school was a success. Elizabeth wrote Antonio, "It is proposed to ... begin on a small plan admitting of enlargement if necessary, in the hope and expectation that there will not be wanting ladies to join in forming a permanent institution," referring to the Sulpicians idea of establishing the Sisters of Charity.

On December 8, 1808, Cecelia O'Conway arrived in Baltimore and became Elizabeth's first spiritual daughter, the first American Sister of Charity. She is sometimes referred to as Philadelphia's first nun.

Elizabeth became Mother Seton on March 25, 1809, when she pronounced private vows of chastity and obedience before Archbishop Carroll, binding for one year.

Elizabeth, Cecilia O'Conway, Maria Murphy, Mary Ann Butler and Susan Clossy donned their religious attire on June 1, 1809, shortly before Elizabeth headed for Emmitsburg.

The Sisters of Charity

The Sisters of Charity of St. Joseph's began its community life on July 31, 1809. The first candidates to join the Sisters of Charity were, Sarah and Ellen Thompson, siblings who lived on a farm near Emmitsburg. Dubourg was the first director. He resigned within a month because he was offended that Mother Seton would protest what she felt was an arbitrary decision of his to the archbishop.

Father John Baptist David was the next director, but his leadership nearly destroyed the community. According to Dirvin, David "took full charge of the affairs of the community, leaving very little to the discretion or direction of Mother Seton and her Council. David's acts were to harass the good Mother, divide the community and almost destroy it throughout the first two crucial years of its existence."

David sought to replace Mother Seton with a protégé of his, Rose Landry White. Mother Seton referred each crisis to the archbishop who chose not to support David.

Archbishop Carroll told her, "Let it be your only concern to progress more and more towards the union of your soul with God. … I declare an opinion and belief that its [the community's] ultimate success under God depends on your sacrificing yourself, notwithstanding all the uneasiness and disgust you may experience, and continuing in your place of Superior."

Mother Seton did continue despite personal trials. Both sisters-in-law, Harriet Seton, died on December 22, 1809, and Cecelia Seton died on April 29, 1810. Her daughter Anna Maria died on March 12, 1812, and her other daughter Rebecca died November 3, 1816, both after struggling against tuberculosis.

David left on May 12, 1811, to help Bishop Benedict Flaget establish the church in Kentucky and John Dubois became the director, to the pleasure of Mother Seton.

Archbishop John Carroll ratified the rule of the sisterhood on January 17, 1812. Both the sisterhood and St. Joseph's Academy and Free School, which the sisters ran, saw success. The accommodations were expanded to St. Joseph's

House (the "White House") to house all of the students seeking admission.

The sisters continued in the face of physical and financial hardships and death as tuberculosis took life after life from among them. Even when consumption finally attacked Mother Seton, she continued her efforts.

Father Simon Gabriel Brute' wrote that Mother Seton was "a true pattern to her Sisters: their mother for love, their servant for humility, their true superior for prudent guidance, their friend in every pain they felt."

St. Joseph's also gained the reputation as an excellent school under Mother Seton's guidance. Dirvin wrote, "She was herself a born teacher: she not only imparted information; she explained it, not once but in several different ways; she illustrated it with examples as simple as the Gospel parables; and she showed where it logically led and what it meant to the learner."

As the administrator of the school, she had her sisters teaching in areas where they were qualified and hired lay teachers to fill the gaps. She visited the classes daily. She also taught religious classes.

St. Joseph's Academy was the first free Catholic school for girls staffed by sisters in the country. Besides boarders, it took in day students from Emmitsburg. From this small school, the Catholic education evolved across the United States leading to the establishment of the parochial school system late in the nineteenth century. For this, Seton is popularly known as a patron of Catholic schools.

The sisterhood assumed management of their first orphanage in 1814 in Philadelphia and a second in 1817 in New York. By the end of 1818, the Philadelphia orphanage had been enlarged to include a free school for German-speaking children.

Elizabeth Ann Seton died on January 4, 1821, at the age of 46.

Besides the school and sisterhood she founded in life, Elizabeth Ann Seton's legacy includes six communities of religious women. The sisters of these communities serve in schools, social ministries and hospitals in America, Korea, and elsewhere around the globe.

In 1963, Pope John XXIII said of Elizabeth, "In a house that was very small, but with ample space for charity, she sowed a seed in America which by Divine Grace grew into a large tree."

The minor basilica and shrine of Saint Elizabeth Ann Seton. Photo courtesy of Wikimedia Commons.

Seton as saint and patroness

Archbishop James Gibbons of Baltimore began Seton's Cause for Canonization on August 22, 1882, after celebrating the Eucharist in the mortuary chapel that housed her remains.

Following years of hearing testimonies of holiness, studying her life and writings, and approval of the miracles for her sainthood, the initiative of prayers was answered.

Pope Paul VI said in 1975, "Elizabeth Ann Seton is a saint. She is the first daughter of the United States of America to be glorified with this incomparable attribute."

In 2006, she also became the patroness of Maryland as designated by the Congregation for Divine Worship and Discipline of Sacraments.

Cardinals Theodore E. McCormick of Washington and William Keeler of Baltimore petitioned the congregation for the decree.

"Mother Seton deserves the title for a multitude of reasons," Cardinal Keeler said. "1. She was the first American citizen to be named a saint. 2. She founded the first Catholic elementary school in Baltimore in 1808 before moving up to Emmitsburg and starting a school there in 1809 and 3. She founded the first community of religious women native to our country."

The shrine to the first American-born saint in includes a museum, basilica, a cemetery and historical homes and draws about 50,000 visitors into the area annually. Docents are on hand in each area to answer questions.

MONSTERS AND MAYHEM

The Hunt for the Snallygaster

S cotland has Nessie, and the American Northwest has Bigfoot. They are legendary monsters. The Middletown Valley has its own monster called the snallygaster.

Snallygasters have been reported in Maryland for centuries. Some people believe the name has German origins. "Schnelle geist" means "fast ghost."

Initially, snallygasters were reptilian birds that preyed on poultry and children.

Frederick County's snallygaster is decidedly nastier.

On February 12, 1909, folks around Middletown, Md., opened their newspapers to read that a large winged creature had swooped down and carried off a man walking along the road. The beast then sucked out most of the man's blood and tossed the empty carcass aside.

"And either the folks in Western Maryland were unusually impressionable or there really was something terrible on the loose, because within hours of the first appearance in the Register, people in Frederick and Washington Counties and even nearby Shepherdstown, West Virginia, began reporting encounters with the flying monster," Susan Fair wrote in *Legends and Lore of Western Maryland*. A man from Casstown, Ohio, wrote in the same issue and called the creature a snallygaster.

Descriptions vary, but once you saw it, you would definitely remember it. Dragonlike, long wings, long pointed tail, sometimes with a horn, one eye in the middle of its forehead, octopus-like tentacles that trailed behind like streamers, re-

43

tractable claws. Some reports noted that the claws were razor sharp. One woman said the snallygaster had hoofs. A man named George Jacobs said he shot at the snallygaster while hunting. Fair wrote, "…the monster apparently didn't care for being shot at. As a matter of fact, it was so annoyed that it pursued Jacobs across a field, all the while lunging angrily—or perhaps hungrily—at the terrified man's neck."

An artist's depiction of the snallygaster.
Courtesy of Wikimedia Commons.

The *Hagerstown Mail* said that the Smithsonian Institution wanted to examine the creature. The *Middletown Valley Register* reported that the military was sending in soldiers armed with Gatling guns.

President Theodore Roosevelt was said to be considering a big-game hunt in Africa to stalk an even greater prize in the snallygaster.

People around Middletown were terrified. Harry Wachtel of Myersville, Md., shot and wounded what he thought was the snallygaster.

It turned out to be a large owl.

"Some say it is a Canadian owl, some say it is just a 'booby owl,' but all agree that with its weird gray wings spread in the cold dead of night it would be taken for a 'snallygaster,' 'jabberwock,' 'wampdoodle' or another terrifying species," the *Frederick Post* reported.

The snallygaster appeared throughout the Middletown Valley, on South Mountain, on Catoctin Mountain, and even as far west as Cumberland, Md., where the snallygaster spoke for the first time.

It reportedly attacked a man there and said, "My, I'm dry! I haven't had a good drink since I was killed in the Battle of Chickamauga." With that report, people started wondering if the creature was a reincarnated Civil War soldier.

In Sharpsburg, Md., it was reported that the nest of eggs from the creature was found.

In Emmitsburg, Md., the creature supposedly tried to grab Ed Brown, a worker on the Emmitsburg Railroad. The beast caught him, but lucky for Brown, his suspender snapped, and he got away. A mob pursued the snallygaster, which then displayed a new skill—shooting fire from its nostrils.

This was the last sighting of the snallygaster for 23 years. In November 1932, reports of the snallygaster began again and even received some national attention. This time, there weren't reports of attacks, but people were scared just the same.

A Canadian owl, which was mistaken for the snallygaster once, and may have actually been the source of the stories. Photo courtesy of Wikimedia Commons.

On December 21, the *Hagerstown Morning Herald* ran the headline: "Death of Snallygaster is reported: Accounts Differ." The newspaper article stated, "The snallygaster circled for sometime above a 2,500-gallon vat, apparently attracted by the fumes. Finally, however, the fumes became too strong, and the creature fell directly into the mash."

A revenue agent and Washington County deputy were supposedly raiding the still around the same time and found the monster, not the bootleggers, who had fled at the sight of the snallygaster.

George Danforth, the revenue agent, was quoted as saying, "Imagine our feeling when our eyes feasted on the monster submerged in the liquor vat."

Apparently, lye in the mash vat supposedly ate away the snallygaster's flesh.

"The remains of the snallygaster were lost to science when Danforth—carrying out his prohibition duties—order the vat and contents destroyed with a large charge of dynamite," the *Cumberland Evening Times* reported.

A few years after the snallygaster's death, another one was reportedly seen in the Middletown Valley area. This one was smaller, though.

"Those who believe that the young monster is a small snallygaster, claim that the unusual heat of the present summer caused one of the eggs to hatch prematurely," the *Hagerstown Daily Mail* wrote.

The article also noted that scientists claimed that it took 15 to 20 years for snallygaster eggs to hatch so if the new snallygaster was an offspring of the one that had died in the moonshine vat, its offspring weren't expected to put in an appearance until 1949 at the earliest.

And so, the legend of the snallygaster continued.

Fair suggests that the story of the snallygaster was inspired by stories of a similar creature called the Jersey Devil. The snallygaster put in its appearance shortly after that.

Some thought the creature was created to scare hobos and vagabonds from Middletown.

Thomas Harbaugh was the Ohio man who first referenced the snallygaster. He was a native of Middletown, though. He was also the author of 650 "nickel novels." I guess they were only half as good as dime novels. He was also good friends with the *Register* editor, George Rhoderick.

"All it took was one little story, and local residents—not to mention reporters and editors of competing newspapers—were ready to release their inner monsters, collaborating on a creation that gleefully took on a life of its own," Fair suggested.

Catoctin Furnace vs. Thurmont

I n September of 1838, a Mechanicstown, Md. (present-day Thurmont, Md.), resident wrote a letter to the editor of the *Baltimore Gazette and Daily Advertiser.*

He told the following story. Earlier that month, shortly before sundown around a dozen employees of Catoctin Furnace had had too much to drink. They came into town with two slaves for the purpose of "using up people."

The men started a fight with two townspeople. "The people, anxious to persevere the peace, and apprehending the consequence of their remaining in town used every means to persuade them from the place. They, however, refused to go and became more violent, until at length one of the citizens, after in vain urging a Negro fellow to throw away some stones with which he had armed himself attempted to take them from him by force; this the Negro resented, with violence, and the citizen knocked him down," the newspaper reported.

Apparently when at least one of these people tried to get back to his house, the furnace mob followed him with clubs and knives "invading and disturbing the peace and quiet of his family, compelling him to escape through a window to which fortunate circumstance probably he owned his life," according to the letter writer.

The town constable got involved and arrested the slaves and imprisoned them. However, the furnace workers instituted a jailbreak and freed them.

The letter writer said, "This act, though highly outrageous, the people were disposed to tolerate, as some of the rioters proposed to depart, and here it was thought the matter would end. We were, however, disappointed. Some one demanded more whiskey, and this the landlord refused to give, supposing no doubt, that they already had too much, and dreading the consequence of giving them more. Upon this, one of them left the crowd, but returned in a moment with an axe, swearing that the landlord who refused to sell liquor ought to have his sign post cut down, & accordingly commended hewing at the post."

Finally, the people in town had had enough and fought back. One of the citizens tried to pull the axe away from the worker and received a severe blow. Suddenly, people were arming themselves with stones, bricks, bats or whatever they could grab.

The workers were eventually driven out of town "some of them so severely beaten that they could not reach the furnace, though but three miles distant, without having their wounds dressed," according to the letter writer.

Interestingly, the letter writer noted that it was a good thing that the slaves left before the fighting began. He said that he had no doubt that if they had gotten swept up in the fight, they would have been killed.

Once the workers were driven out of town, residents appointed guards to patrol the streets. At the close of the letter, the writer pointed out that the people of Mechanicstown were peaceful and hardworking, but "any attempt to disturb the people hereafter, in a similar manner will be opposed by an *efficient force well prepared for the purpose.*"

The story shows that there was tension between the blue-collar laborers and slaves of the furnace and the small businessmen and farmers of Mechanicstown.

A unique aspect of this story is that slaves stood with

furnace workers during the fight. The white workers even rescued the slaves from jail.

An 1890 view that shows the Catoctin Furnace ironworks, the supply store, and the manor house. Photo courtesy of Thurmontimages.com.

The Wreck of the Blue Mountain Express

On June 25, 1915, the Blue Mountain Express bound for Hagerstown, Md., pulled into the Western Maryland Railroad Station in Thurmont about 20 minutes late for its 5:10 p.m. stop in town. Apparently, the train had had a hotbox that needed to be repacked while the train was in Union Bridge, Md., according to Charles Eyler in George Wireman's book, *Gateway to the Mountains.*

In Thurmont, the train hurriedly took on water and dropped off Baltimore's afternoon newspapers for delivery. The stop was short in hopes of making up some lost time.

The express was made up of a Pullman Parlor Car, three coaches, and a baggage car. "Although it was primarily a freight line, the Western Maryland became famous for the excursion trains it ran to the Blue Ridge, and for the Blue Mountain Express, said to have been the finest train in the East," Wireman wrote.

Meanwhile, in Hagerstown, the train dispatcher, Edgar Bloom, was busy trying to keep trains moving along the stretch of track that he watched over. Of the 180 miles under his supervision, all but 20 miles was single track. That meant if two trains were coming from different directions, he had to notify the nearest station to have one train pull off onto a siding until the other train passed.

Bloom had been doing this for a while and knew his job, but today, he was having trouble communicating to the east.

A storm earlier in the week had knocked down a telegraph line. Add to that, the general confusion of a hectic day and Bloom lost track of countermanding an order that gave the Blue Mountain Express the right of way, according to the *Adams County News.*

From Thurmont, the next stop was Sabillasville, Md. Outside of Thurmont, the Blue Mountain Express started up the mountain on a section of single track that ran for just over two miles.

Around 5:30 p.m., local residents heard the familiar sound of the Blue Mountain Express's train whistle, but instead of stopping, it continued blowing. People knew something was the matter and rushed to where they heard the whistle.

On the tracks, it's not certain how soon the engineers saw the trouble coming at them. The eastbound Baltimore Unlimited came head to head with the westbound Blue Mountain Express.

"It is presumed that the engineers of both trains believed the other had been ordered to take the siding to allow his train to pass.", all-steel cars helped minimize loss of life," the *Adams County News* reported.

The two engines hit. The impact crumpled some cars and knocked others off the High Bridge over Owens Creek into the ravine 100 feet below.

Seconds before the crash, Fireman Vendergerst on the Baltimore Unlimited "made a thrilling leap for safety," according to the *Frederick News*. It did him little good. He was found later with a broken back and legs broken in several places. He was taken to the hospital in Hagerstown.

R. B. Taylor of Westminster, Md., was sitting in the smoking car when he felt the train slowing. He thought the engineer might be applying the emergency brake.

"I thrust my head out of the window and beheld a terrifying sight," Taylor told the *Hagerstown Herald-Mail*. "The engine and tender of the Blue Mountain was over the bridge, while the baggage car was smashed in, part of it falling into the ravine behind the engine and tender."

Uninjured, Taylor grabbed his things and headed for the door along with the other passengers in the car.

He was one of the lucky ones.

The Blue Mountain Express on High Bridges on June 24, 1915. Only the eastbound engine is visible. The westbound engine had already been removed by this time. Photo courtesy of Thurmontimages.com.

Thomas B. South of Hagerstown was in the passenger car next to the baggage car that crashed into the ravine. He felt a "grating sensation before the crash came." The impact threw him forward against the seat in front of him.

"Mr. South said he could feel the car in which he was riding turn almost completely around and that it then tilted, as if it was going into the ravine," reported the *Hagerstown*

Herald-Mail. "Women screamed and children cried when the awful compact came, and great difficulty was experienced in getting them out of the cars."

Harry Smith of Hagerstown was seated in a passenger car of the Blue Mountain Express and "he felt the car topple and pieces of glass flew in every direction and many persons were badly cut," according to the *Hagerstown Herald-Mail*.

The two trains hit head-on. The baggage car on the Blue Mountain Express fell into the ravine, carrying with it two passengers, Mrs. W. C. Chipchase and her son, Walter.

"Mrs. Chipchase was going to be admitted to a sanitarium, was reclining in a baggage car, son and nurse with her, the nurse left to stroll through the train, which probably saved her," the *Adams County News* reported.

Mrs. Chipchase died in the fall, but Walter was found unconscious and groaning when rescuers reached him.

The *Frederick News* reported that Walter was taken to a cottage at Blue Ridge Summit, Pa., where his sister Ethel had been waiting for her brother and mother to arrive. He died around midnight.

The engines of the two trains had locked together on impact, "appearing as almost one engine to the horrified rescuers who quickly gathered on the scene. Had the engines ricocheted off of one another, there undoubtedly would have been more causalities," according to a historical study of Catoctin National Park.

Wireman wrote, "Coals were falling from one of the boilers and for a time threatened to set fire to the wooden structure of the bridge. The whistle on one of the engines had stuck in an open position and kept blowing until all of the steam was gone."

Within minutes of the crash, about 100 people had gathered to help the survivors and find the dead amid the debris.

As the passengers and crew were located and pulled from the wreckage, two bodies were seen that could not be reached easily. Fireman Hayes' body was hanging from the train's cab, but no one could reach it because the cab was hung over the ravine.

"It was impossible to move the body for fear that the slightest motion would hurl it to the bottom of the ravine nearly 100 feet below," the *Frederick News* reported.

Dr. Morris Birely of Thurmont was the first doctor on the scene. He went to work treating the wounded as best he could. He worked into the night using gas lanterns for light.

The Western Maryland Railroad sent two special trains to help in transporting the dead and wounded from the area. One train came from the east and the other the west.

All of the wreckage except the connected locomotives had been cleared from the bridge by morning.

"People were still wondering the next day how the two engines had stayed on the rails. But it was easy to see how the wreck had occurred. The bridge is 'blind' from both directions. From the east, a train passes out of a deep, curving cut right onto the bridge. From the west, an engineer had a little more visibility but was also on a curve and was traveling down-hill, making a quick stop impossible," Wireman wrote.

In the end, six died in the crash of the Blue Mountain Express. They were: Coleman Cook, engineer; Luther Hull, fireman; J. R. Hayes, fireman; Mrs. W. C. Chipchase, Baltimore; Walter Chipchase, Baltimore. Twelve others suffered severe injuries. An investigation revealed that a mix-up in the all-important right-of-way orders issued from Hagerstown had caused the crash.

Bloom "Pale and worn, the unmistakable signs of the worry he has experienced since hearing the result of his mistake," according to the *Adams County News*, accepted responsibility for the accident.

Oddly, there were three Western Maryland Railroad officials on the Blue Mountain Express on their way to a meeting about preventing wrecks.

The wreck of the Blue Mountain Express on June 24, 1915. This picture was altered at some point to make it appear as if the engines are touching. You can see that part of the photograph has been cut out. Photo courtesy of Thurmontimages.com.

Did One Death Lead to Six?

What if there was another contributing factor in the accident no one realized because it had happened months earlier?

William H. Webb was a 65-year-old watchman on the bridges west of Thurmont. Each day, he would walk to his shanty next to the bridges from his home on Kelbaugh Road. Every day, his wife, Sarah, would have one of their children or grandchildren take William his lunch.

"As watchman of those bridges, Mr. Webb's position was an important one. The safety of many passengers and trains depended upon his watchfulness during the hours of the night. He walked those bridges at regular intervals during all hours of the night," the *Frederick Post* reported.

William H. Webb, the man who might have been able to prevent the wreck of the Blue Mountain Express. Photo courtesy of Roger Troxell.

By 1915, he'd been an employee of the Western Maryland Railroad for 35 years. His job was isolated, but he enjoyed it.

Webb was Roger Troxell's great-grandfather. According to stories that his mother told him, "One of the children or grandchildren took him his lunch one day. It was pouring down rain and he found him (Webb) sitting on the railing holding his umbrella, and he was dead."

This differs from the accounts in the *Frederick Post* and *Catoctin Clarion*. They reported that the day watchman had found William lying beside the cross-tie block on February 24, 1915.

"When found his overcoat was drawn up over his shoulders, and a raised umbrella lay beside him," the *Frederick Post* reported.

The *Catoctin Clarion* explained that it appeared as if Webb had come east from his shack across the iron bridge to "signal" the Fast Mail train going west soon after 6 o'clock, and while walking to his post east of the bridge was stricken with heart trouble and died.

The day watchman telephoned to Thurmont, and Dr. Birely and Magistrate E. E. Black came out to the bridges to examine the body. No marks were found on it, and Birely said that heart failure was the cause of death.

Although this was months before the summer wreck of the Blue Mountain Express, there's no indication that another watchman was hired to replace Webb. Also, one of the trains that wrecked was the fast mail train that Webb usually signaled.

Had Webb still been alive and on the job, he may have been able to signal the trains to stop before they wrecked on the bridges. Bloom may also have been able to call the shanty directly about the mix-up rather than telegraphing a message to the Western Maryland Railroad Station in Thurmont and hope to stop the train before it left the station.

Where Did the Dwayyo Away Go?

W
as it a man or beast, and just where did the name Dwayyo come from?

At the end of November 1965, John Becker heard a noise in his backyard. When he went to investigate and found a six-foot-tall creature covered in black fur with a bushy tail. The two fought and the beast ran off.

Becker called the Maryland State Police to report the creature, calling it a Dwayyo. Besides what the beast was, the origin of the name was never explained.

Becker told the police that he lived on Fern Rock Road, a narrow dirt road near the entrance of Gambrill State Park. The police tried to investigate the call, but they couldn't find a John Becker in Frederick County or a Fern Rock Road.

Most people assumed the call was a prank or that the man had had too much to drink and was seeing things. However, a couple days later, a Frederick man was hunting near Middletown and had a run in with a creature.

"My dogs started chasing something, and I saw it was black, but I didn't think too much of it, believing it was a dog maybe even a bear," he told George May with the *Frederick Post.* "However, after reading the newspaper article, I'm not too sure it wasn't a Dwayyo. It trotted something like a horse. I don't know what it was, but I'm looking for it this week."

Most people were skeptical of the story, but some began to

worry. It didn't help that May continued to write about the mysterious creature. Even though it was obvious he was one of the skeptics, some of his readers weren't.

When police went to investigate a report that someone had been holding the Dwayyo captive in his basement for a year, not only didn't they find the Dwayyo, but the property owner said he hadn't called the police. May wrote, "The City Police went to a basement to get themselves a Dwayyo; but when they got there the basement was bare and the Dwayyo had gone away-yo."

An Ellerton, Md., woman reported that she may have heard the Dwayyo months earlier near her Catoctin Mountain home. "It cried like a baby and then screamed like a woman for months. All our neighbors heard it. My husband tried to look for footprints, but none could be found."

In man near Middletown, Md., called in a report, saying that he had seen the Dwayyo and that it looked like a dog. In fact, several people called saying that the artist sketch in the newspaper reminded them of an Irish Wolfhound on its hind legs. The breed can stand three feet high on more when on all fours and weigh upwards from 120 pounds.

Some people also began suggested it might be a snally-gaster, the other famous monster from Middletown Valley. However, the two descriptions were nothing alike.

A hunt was planned for the Dwayyo that supposedly 100 people signed up for. However, it didn't happen because too few people showed up.

"A young Frederick boy, apparently worried about the Dwayyo, said he thought the paper was just making –up the Dwayyo stories so children would be good until Christmas," May wrote in one of his stories.

The tipping point seemed to be when a letter for John Becker arrived at the Frederick News-Post offices in care of

May. The letter was from the Frederick County Treasurer and contained a dog license for the Dwayyo.

After that, sightings stopped, and May suggested that perhaps the creature had moved on.

Many people believed the Dwayyo could have been an Irish Wolfhound. Photo courtesy of Wikimedia Commons.

The Phantoms and Monsters blog reported that the Dwayyo was seen the following year again just outside of Gambrill State Park. A man known only as Jim A. saw it as he headed for his campsite. "It was described as a shaggy two legged creature the size of a deer that had a triangle shaped head with pointed ears and chin. It was dark brown in color and when approached it made a horrid scream and backed away from the man. Jim described it as having an odd walk as it retreated, its legs, 'stuck out from the side of the trunk of the body making its movements appear almost spider-like as it backed away'".

Ten years later, two men were on Catoctin Mountain on a private road between Cunningham Falls State Park and Catoctin Mountain Park. A large animal ran across the road in front of them, and they saw it in their headlights. Their description matched the general description of the Dwayyo.

If the Dwayyo had moved on, as May suggested in 1965, then it hadn't gone far, just moving north along Catoctin Mountain.

Maybe it will make another appearance, or it may continue to be just as elusive as Bigfoot.

TOP SECRET

A Place to Rest and Recover

A lthough the United States didn't enter World War II until December 1941, it was showing favorites in the fighting before then. One such instance was when the U.S. government invited British sailors to Catoctin Mountain to rest up and relax from the strain and stress of war.

The Catoctin Recreational Demonstration Area had three summer camps with recreational facilities at the start of the war, and it was in an out-of-the-way location where they sailors wouldn't draw attention.

The U.S. Secretary of the Navy granted permission for British sailors to use the camps to relax on June 2, 1941. These camps provided "a tremendous amount of good to personnel who had many months of arduous sea duty," according to the Catoctin Mountain Park website.

Known as Project 119, Catoctin Mountain began hosting 74 British sailors on June 10, 1941. They stayed anywhere from a single day to several weeks. "The men were provided living and sleeping quarters as well as use of all facilities in Camp #2 [Camp Greentop] including the swimming pool," according to the website.

The U.S. Navy provided the food, which Royal Navy cooks prepared. Besides Camp #2, the sailors also used the Civilian Conservations Corps camp, Camp #1, and Mt. Lent.

By the time, the project was ended in November of 1941, 630 Royal Navy sailors had made use of the facilities on Catoctin Mountain.

Although it stopped hosting British sailors, this did not end Catoctin Mountain's use as a place for servicemen to rest and recover.

In 1942, representatives from the National Park Service and park hotel and restaurant operators met for two days to talk about military use of the national parks for "morale, welfare and recreation."

A British sailor relaxes on his bunk in a cabin at Camp Misty Mount. Photo courtesy of the Catoctin Mountain Park photo archives.

"In wartime, the best function of these areas is to prove a place to which members of the armed forces and civilians may retire to restore shattered nerves and to recuperate physically and mentally for the war tasks still ahead of them," said Newton Drury, who was the wartime NPS Director.

The Catoctin Mountain Park website also points out that the parties had secondary motives. The NPS hoped that by using the national parks for recreational uses, the military would stop trying to use them as training areas. The vendors hoped that their empty bed and lagging sales would change for the better. (The war had severely reduced the number of visitors to national parks because of rationing of gasoline and rubber.) The War Department hoped it would find an inexpensive place for servicemen to stay.

An agreement was reached, and parks like Carlsbad Caverns, Denali, and the Grand Canyon became favorite recreational sites.

At Catoctin Mountain Park, U.S. Marines recovering and resting from their ordeals at Iwo Jima and Okinawa in the Pacific came to Camp Greentop, which has previously been used by the OSS, in 1945. Because the OSS has stopped using Area B in 1944, the Marines didn't have to hear the sound of gunfire, which could have triggered a post-traumatic stress reaction.

Spies On the Mountain

T he sailors who were getting specialized training at Miami University in Ohio gathered in the campus auditorium. They waited uncertainly, not knowing what to expect since their training was not yet done.

Lieutenant Greene walked onto the stage and asked the group if anyone could speak a foreign language. Hands rose among the sailors in the audience.

Spiro Cappony's hand was among those that went up. He was a young 19-year old who had become so caught up in patriotic fervor after watching the movie "Wake Island" that he enlisted in the U.S. Navy to fight for his country. And as a first-generation American, he could speak the language of his parents, Greek.

Cappony and other sailors who had raised their hands were separated from the main group and interviewed. Once the interviewer found out Cappony spoke Greek, he asked, "Would you like to try something different?" Cappony recalled during a November 2007 phone interview.

"What?" Cappony asked the interviewer.

"Would you like to become a paratrooper?"

Unsure of what he had heard, Cappony said, "I'm in the Navy, sir."

The interviewer nodded. "Well, this is something different. It's a special training course."

"If I have to, I have to," Cappony said, shrugging.

So began Cappony's journey as an agent for the Office of Strategic Services, the forerunner of the Central Intelligence

Agency, during WWII.

The OSS

"The Office of Strategic Services was the first effort by this country at unorthodox warfare and strategic intelligence. Prior to that time, the army and navy had what we called tactical intelligence that had to do with battlefield intelligence and the like, but [William] Donovan felt and convinced the president that we had to know what the capabilities and the intentions of other nations were from a strategic point of view," William Putzell, Jr. said in his interview for the Library of Congress's Veterans History Project.

The seal of the Office of Strategic Services. Courtesy of the CIA.

Donovan was a highly decorated veteran who had gone into a private law practice until President Franklin D. Roosevelt called him back to serve his country and put together the new intelligence-gathering unit.

"He's [Donovan's] the only one in my limited experience that had physical and intellectual daring in one person. You usually see one or the other but not both," Putzell said.

At its peak in late 1944, the OSS employed nearly 13,000 civilians and military personnel, according to the CIA website. About 7,500 of them served overseas, and approximately 4,500 of the employees were women (and 900 of them served overseas). Over its four-year life, the OSS spent about $135 million or more than $1 billion in current dollars to gather enemy intelligence and disrupt their operations.

Recruits arrive at the OSS training camp on Catoctin Mountain. Screenshot from an OSS film.

Catoctin Recreational Demonstration Area

The OSS maintained training camps in Virginia, Maryland, and Canada. The Maryland site was located on Catoctin Mountain in Frederick County, Md. The location was about an hour north of Washington, D.C. and next door to President Roosevelt's retreat that he called Shangri-La.

The Catoctin Recreational Demonstration Area had been a popular summer camp for groups like the League for Crippled Children and The Salvation Army. On April 5, 1942, the swing arm gates of the park swung shut and were locked. A notice ran in the newspapers notifying readers, "The Catoctin Area is Ordered Closed to the Public." Armed guards stood watch to make sure they stayed that way. Once the gates were closed, former Catoctin Mountain Park Ranger Debra Mills said those groups were "given notice that the summer camping season was canceled and no future use could be guaranteed."

The residents of Frederick County had become used to a military presence on Catoctin Mountain. In the summer of 1941, a temporary training camp had been set up in the Catoctin Recreational Demonstration Area and soldiers set up their tents next to the CCC barracks already on the mountain. British sailors also enjoyed a break from the war and used the park for recreation, according to national park records.

Although Catoctin Mountain Park was leased to the War Department, "The park superintendents remained on duty to continue the National Park Service's primary mission: to preserve the natural resources for future generations of Americans. Under the terms of the lease, the War Department agreed to uphold the Park's prohibitions on the destruction of trees, shrubs, and wildlife, and to restore the Park's facilities at the end of the war," John Whiteclay Chambers, II, wrote in *Catoctin History*.

Because of the government's need for training camps, it had turned to the National Park Service and, in particular, recreation demonstration areas for land to create temporary camps. RDAs were generally located near urban areas and had camp facilities in them, but they were still primitive enough that having thousands of men tramp over them wouldn't cause permanent damage.

Then trains began arriving and stopping at Lantz, Md., to unload men and women who entered the guarded camp. Others began arriving by truck.

"We got into a truck in Washington (D.C.) that had the side flaps down. We didn't know where we were going," Frank Gleason said during an October 2007 phone interview. Gleason had been a demolitions instructor at Area B.

Most of the recruits arriving at Area B had already completed preliminary training at another OSS camp in what is currently Prince William Forest Park in Virginia.

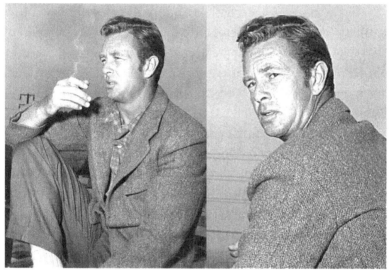

Actor Sterling Hayden was an OSS agent who trained at Catoctin Mountain Park. Photo courtesy of Wikimedia Commons.

The Recruits

Military recruits like Cappony and Gleason were the people the OSS usually recruited, but that was not always the case. Chambers said many young men were recruited from top universities and society families to be trained as spies. However, to learn needed skills, they mixed with criminals who taught things like safecracking and forgery.

Women were also among the recruits. "The women, most of them that became -- went into the Secret Service were

American citizens, but they had backgrounds of French or English or German. And so it was very easy to give them a passport, again, of that nationality. So technically, no, no American woman went into combat or went into the intelligence, parachuted in. But in actuality, they did," Former OSS agent Rafael Hirtz said in his interview for the National History Project.

Area B

Major Ainsworth Blogg was the first commander of Area B. The OSS had recruited him from the Army Reserves around the same time that the park was closed to the public.

Recruits working out on the trainazium. Screenshot from the OSS film about Area B.

Camp Greentop was used as a training school, and the administrative center was located in Camp Round Meadow.

Both of these used existing facilities. Some specialized facilities, such as firing ranges and obstacle courses, needed to be constructed to turn the national park into a place that could train recruits in a basic paramilitary course.

One unique obstacle course was called a "trainazium." Six telephone-pole-size logs were set into the ground and connected by smaller poles 18 feet above the ground. An old film of the trainazium shows recruits swinging, running, and climbing a the top of the trainazium.

Gleason was quoted in *Catoctin History* as saying, the trainazium was used "to build the men's self-confidence, to build up their physical strength and dexterity...and [teach them] to be agile on narrow high places."

Another unique training feature camp was called the "House of Horrors." It was a windowless building "filled with wobbly walkways, moving objects, sound effects, flashing lights, and other surprises," Chambers wrote. Trainees, armed with a .45-caliber pistol and two clips of six rounds, were sent into the house at night. As the trainees crept through the house, cardboard cutouts of Nazis popped into the open, requiring trainees to think fast and shoot them, according to the Catoctin Mountain Park website.

Edgar Prichard, a recruit at Area B, said in *Catoctin History*, "Each of us over a period of a couple of days would be awakened in the middle of the night and hauled off to carry out a special mission. When it came my time, I was told that there was a Nazi soldier holed up in a building and that it was my job to go in and kill him. I was given a .45 and two clips [of ammunition]. The house I was sent into was a log house with long corridors and stairways. I wasn't sure whether there really was a Nazi soldier there or not. I kicked a door open with my gun at the ready. Paper targets with photographs of uniformed German soldiers jumped out at me from every corner and every window and doorway. We had been taught to always fire two shots at the target. There must have been six targets because I got two bullets in each one. The last one was a dummy sitting in a chair with a lighted cigarette in his hand. If you didn't shoot him you failed the test."

The House of Horrors at Area B. Screenshot from the OSS film about Area B.

Area B instructors like Gleason trained OSS agents in hand-to-hand combat, infiltration training, marksmanship and setting charges. Other instruction included creating disguises, concealing microfilm, and recruiting resistance agents. "Students tested different explosives and fuses on pieces of iron, steel, and wood as practice for blowing up bridges, dams, railroad radio towers or power plants," Chambers wrote.

"We trained in individual sabotage," Gleason said. "It's what the terrorists do now. It was fascinating work. Our job was to interfere with the enemy in every way possible."

At any given time, the camp would have about 100 recruits who were spending two weeks in training on the mountain, according to the Catoctin Mountain Park website. However, the site could accommodate up to 250 trainees, plus staff, according to Chambers who based his estimate on layout maps of the buildings in the camp.

Cappony said that one of the first assignments he was given when he arrived at Area B was to "bust up rocks like we were convicts. It was a test of our endurance and our minds to see if they could get to us."

Cappony's training allowed him to pack on muscle until he weighed 180 pounds.

"I became a tough, little guy," he said. "I learned about knife throwing, how to kill with my bare hands, how to kill with a newspaper or a comb."

Cappony trained with the man who had recruited him into the OSS, Captain John Hamilton. By the time they arrived at Area B, Cappony already knew that John Hamilton was actually movie actor Sterling Hayden. He would also go on to fight the Germans in Yugoslavia.

"We didn't know anyone by their real names," said Albert Guay in a November 2007 phone interview. He worked as a company clerk at Area B for a few months.

During training, none of the recruits used their real names—even to those in their group. Instead, aliases allowed for a cloak of secrecy. Among the expert training staff was a colorful English colonel, formerly employed by the Shanghai police. The colonel was remembered as a particularly "notorious character in the OSS," according to the Catoctin Mountain Park website.

Recruits were sometimes injured during training. In one incident, trainees were told to crawl along a path as small explosions detonated overhead, simulating combat. According to Chambers, William Casey, a young lawyer from New

York, rose up too soon.

"An explosion knocked a piece of wood from the tree about the size of a football," Chambers said. "It hit him in the face and broke his jaw."

That young trainee grew up to become director of the CIA under President Reagan.

"Many people who later became directors of the CIA had commando training here in Catoctin," Chambers said.

During the 4- to 6-week training course, the trainees' days lasted from 6 a.m. to 11 p.m. with actual training running from 7 a.m. to 5 p.m. six days a week.

"When we were well trained, I could take a group of six people and put a major city out of action for a month," Gleason said. "You blow up the sewers, blow up power plants, and destroy the motors for phones."

American agents weren't the only ones who trained at Area B. Recruits came from Norway, Thailand, Yugoslavia, Italy, and France and went through the rigorous training at Catoctin, according to Chambers.

After completing OSS training, the agents' "final project" was to infiltrate various military targets in the region, such as shipyards and steel mills. According to Chambers, William Peers and Nicol Smith were able to get into the Fairchild Aircraft factory in Hagerstown in 1942 and return not only with the layout of the factory, but with a plan for how to sabotage it.

If the trainees were successful like Peers and Smith, they were sent into the field.

Taking a Break

The trainees weren't always stuck in camp during their training. They traveled to nearby towns for a drink or USO dances where they could enjoy the company of pretty girls.

"They would load us on the truck and take us into Thurmont, Hagerstown, and Frederick on weekends and evenings," Guay said.

When asked where they were from, the soldiers always said Fort Ritchie, which was an army fort north of the OSS camp.

"It was supposed to be a secret, but it didn't take long to know that everyone already knew," Guay said. "It wasn't much of a secret."

Behind Enemy Lines

Once the agents were trained, many of them had their training put to the test when they were sent behind enemy lines.

In 1943, Cappony shipped out to Cairo, Egypt. He did parachute training in Palestine before being sent to work in the embassy in Istanbul, Turkey. While at the embassy, Cappony found out that Turkey was funneling ore to Germany via supply lines. Cappony set out to disrupt those operations. He spent nine months in northern Greece working with Greek guerrillas. They blew up bridges, engaged in counterattacks and did everything they could to harass the Germans.

"I knew I had been trained to protect myself. I was in dangerous territory. I knew I could be mean, quick and protect myself. I knew I had to be good or I'd be dead," Cappony said.

Not all of the agents were successful. Some paid the ultimate price. "In March 1944, all fifteen members of a sabotage team of Italian Americans from the OSS Italian Operational Group that had trained at Area B were caught and executed by the Nazis in an open field in northern Italy," Chambers wrote.

Chambers said his research has led him to believe, "The OSS had a significant role in helping the Allies to win the war."

As for the history of the OSS, information is beginning to dribble out as more and more documents are declassified. With more information available, the men and women of the OSS are being recognized for their service.

Gen. Hap Holliday awards Spiro Cappony the Bronze Star for his actions as an OSS agent. Photo courtesy of the Veterans History Project.

Guay, who got out of the OSS after a few months said, "Looking back I think I made a big mistake. I had no idea what that would turn into."

In 2007, the Greek Embassy honored Cappony and the other agents who served behind enemy lines.

End of the War

The OSS closed Area B in June 1944, and Camp Ritchie took over the training areas to use for its Army Military Intelligence Training School.

Once the war ended, the process of returning the park to civilian use began. Camp Ritchie Army Engineers removed the munitions and firing range and dismantled the House of Horrors and trainazium. They also had to examine the training areas to remove booby traps and unexploded grenades and mortar shells.

Because the heavy traffic on Catoctin Mountain had damaged the main road to the park that was located near Lantz, a new road was constructed. This road was designated Route 77, and a new entrance to the park was built off of it.

Area B Today

Very little remains to show the military's presence in Catoctin Mountain Park. The OSS winterized the camping cabins, and the mountain is now home to a state park, a national park, and Camp David.

"We have found one mortar round that could have been from the training done up here," said former Catoctin Mountain Park Superintendent Mel Poole.

Poole said that it's been known the park was an OSS camp for years, but it has only been in recent years that it has become known what the OSS was.

"I think the real trigger to realizing what went on here was when I went to the International Spy Museum," Poole said. "I was standing next to James Bond's Aston Martin, and they were showing a continuous loop of a film shot here on Catoctin Mountain by [Academy Award-Winning Director] John Ford about what they did here."

The film shows the training of the agents at Area B and even places like the House of Horrors. However, all of the recruits in the movie wear "Lone Ranger" masks so that they can't be identified.

The National Park Service is still trying to piece together the details of life in the camp.

"We always thought people came in by the road they use now," Poole said. "When we took a former agent around, he didn't recognize the place until we went up by Lantz. Then he said, 'This is the way we came and went in the park.'"

Once the former agent was oriented, he was able to identify many of the areas of Area B and explain to the park staff what they had been used for.

Still, not everything is known about Area B's history. Catoctin Mountain Park holds onto some of its secrets just as tightly as the OSS did.

A Presidential Getaway

The Catoctin Mountain area first came to the president's attention when Herbert Hoover visited the area to fish. Then during the Great Depression, the federal government purchased the land to create the Catoctin Recreation Demonstration Area to show how submarginal farmlands and poorly managed forest lands could be converted into a valuable recreational resource.

When WWII started, a portion of the land was dedicated to the OSS training camp, but President Roosevelt wanted a secluded getaway spot. His home in Hyde Park was considered too far away, and rail travel could have been dangerous with enemy agents about.

So the Secret Service began searching for sites that were within two hours of Washington, D.C. by car. The president's doctor also recommended that the location be at least 2000 feet above sea level for coolness and fresh air.

Potential sites were investigated, and the Catoctin Recreation Demonstration Area was selected, and President Roosevelt dubbed his retreat as "Shangri-La." Shangri-La is a fictional place described in the 1933 novel *Lost Horizon* by British author James Hilton. Hilton describes Shangri-La as a mystical, harmonious valley, gently guided from a lamasery, enclosed in the western end of the Kunlun Mountains. Shangri-La has become synonymous with any earthly paradise, and particularly a mythical Himalayan utopia – a permanently happy land, isolated from the outside world.

Although the site remained a secret to most of the world

until after Roosevelt's death in 1945, the citizens of Thurmont knew what was going on.

Roosevelt and Churchill

President Franklin Roosevelt and British Prime Minister fishing at Shangri-La during WWII. Courtesy of the Library of Congress.

Frederick Tresselt, an area goldfish farmer, ran a retail store next to the main north-south road through the county. According to Frederick's son, Ernest, the store had a large pond with a Hunting Creek Fisheries sign in the middle of it. Above the name was a large fantail goldfish painted in bright orange. The area was nicely landscaped with water lilies, shrubs, and bamboo. It was an attractive location and an eye-catching sign, so eye-catching that one Sunday afternoon in

1942, three large, black cars pulled off the road and stopped.

A military man stepped out of the car and Frederick recognized him as General George Marshall, President Franklin Roosevelt's chief of staff. "Mr. Churchill and Mr. Roosevelt and I are interested in seeing your operation here," Marshall said, according to Ernest.

The original sign for the presidential retreat. Photo courtesy of the National Park Service.

Frederick agreed, and the drivers pulled the cars in closer to the fish house, the storage building with concrete pools and wine vats.

"President Roosevelt looked in the door, but he didn't

come in, since he was handicapped and couldn't get out of the car," Ernest Tresselt wrote in his autobiography.

However, Winston Churchill, the prime minister of Great Britain, got out of the car and walked into the fish house with Frederick. They began talking about Tresselt's unique crop. Churchill showed an interest in the golden orfes, which were fifteen to eighteen inches long. Churchill said he had even bigger ones in his pond in England. Tresselt told the prime minister that he, too, had larger fish in his ponds on Hunting Creek Fisheries.

As the cars with Roosevelt and Churchill departed, a Secret Service agent told Frederick not to tell anyone about the visit. "This made no sense to Dad because there were already at least a hundred local people out there taking it all in. But Dad didn't tell anybody, not even us kids," Ernest said. He found out at school the next day when everyone but Ernest seemed to know about the visit of the two world leaders.

A cabinet meeting at Camp David. Photo courtesy of Wikimedia Commons.

Some of the battle plans for WWII were put together between military leaders and the President at Shangri-La.

Changes were also made to improve the look and conveniences available there with each new administration. There are two fully-equipped lodges – Laurel and Aspen – on the compound. Camp David cost $100,000 to maintain in 1945 and somewhere between $1 million and $2 million in 1986. The annual budget is currently around $8.5 million.

Other presidents

Over the years, Shangri-Li would host many world leaders over the years. Some of the foreign guests include Egyptian President Anwar al-Sadat, Israeli Prime Minister Menachem Begin, Indonesian President Suharto, Princess Martha of Norway, Princess Juliana of the Netherlands, French President Charles De Gaulle, British Prime Minister Harold Macmillan, Soviet Premier Nikita Khrushchev, and Australian Prime Minister Harold Holt.

President John F. Kennedy enjoys some time with his children at Camp David. Photo courtesy of the Library of Congress.

President Harry Truman didn't use the retreat often. It is thought that his wife, Bess, found it boring, and Truman apparently believed in the words of a wise man, "If mama ain't happy, ain't nobody happy."

President Dwight Eisenhower often enjoyed the retreat even though he had purchased his farm in Gettysburg, Pa. It was President Eisenhower who renamed Shangri-La Camp David in honor of his grandson. He also held his first cabinet meeting following his heart attack at Camp David on November 22, 1955.

President John F. Kennedy used the retreat, but he enjoyed visiting a seaside retreat more. He also made use Camp David available to his Cabinet members, aides, and their families.

The first wedding at Camp David was in 1992 when President George H. W. Bush's daughter, Dorothy Bush Koch, was married there.

Egyptian President Anwar El Sadat and Israeli Prime Minister

87

Menachem Begin, assisted by President Jimmy Carter, nego-
tiated peace at Camp David in 1978.

Camp David Accords

Perhaps the most significant event to happen at Camp
David was the secret negotiations that took place there in
1978 between Egyptian President Anwar El Sadat and Israeli
Prime Minister Menachem Begin, assisted by President Jimmy Carter. For the 12 days of negotiations on the mountain,
the town of Thurmont was filled with reporters and protesters
who filled up the hotels and camped.

The accords were signed on September 17, 1978. It led to
the Egypt-Israel Peace Treaty in 1979 and a shared Nobel
Peace Prize between Begin and Sadat.

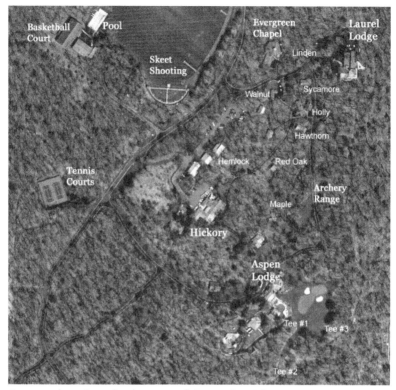

A map showing the layout of Camp David.

Danger at Camp David

Former Thurmont mayor and current commissioner Martin Burns was stationed at Camp David from 1986 to 1989 when he was a Marine.

He said President George H.W. Bush would walk into the camp gym and say "Hey, Marine, wanna play racquetball?"

He also told the *Washington Post* a story about Burt. Burt was Camp David's domesticated deer. Someone donated a bottle-fed spike to Camp David, and during the Reagan years, the deer would prance around, nibbling on sugar cubes and dandelions from Marines' hands, nudging them from behind if he wanted to play.

For all of the protection from external threats that the Marines provide, the real danger came from within. Burt grew into a full-fledged buck and, in a territorial fit, mauled a Marine, sticking one of his antlers four inches deep into the poor man's thigh.

Burt sent off the grounds into the surrounding mountainside and was never seen again.

Gettysburg and Leesburg

It should also be noted that two presidents had homes at either end of Catoctin Mountain. President Dwight D. Eisenhower raised Black Angus cattle his farm in Gettysburg.

Eisenhower and his wife had purchased the farm in 1950 before he became president. Not only did he host world leaders, such as Soviet Premier Nikita Khrushchev, French President Charles de Gaulle, and British Prime Minister Winston Churchill, there as president, but the farm served as a temporary White House for him to conduct the work of the nation when he was recovering from a heart attack.

President James Monroe's Oak Hill mansion and plantation is located just south of Catoctin Mountain below Leesburg.

The 1820 mansion was built during Monroe's presidency, and it was his only residence from 1827 to 1830. He later split his time between Oak Hill and another home at the University of Virginia.

Training the Unemployed From the Catoctin Mountaintop

C atoctin Mountain can boast a lot of fascinating history from Camp David to the Blue Blazes Still raid. From an OSS training camp during World War II to Camp Misty for children.

"Also on the Government side is the 'mother' camp of President Johnson's Poverty Program," the *Frederick Post* reported in 1965.

Before he became president, Johnson had been the Texas director of the National Youth Administration. It was a New Deal program under President Franklin D. Roosevelt similar in objective to the Job Corps. Johnson convinced Congress it could work again, according to Barbara Kirkconnell in *Catoctin Mountain Park, An Administrative History*.

The camp, called Camp Round Meadow, opened in January 1965 and served as the place to train people who would be sent out across the country to depressed areas to open and operate other similar camps.

At the camp, 75 people were hired and trained on how to run a poverty training camp. "While these people are being instructed, some 20 persons accepted as trainees by the new program, will be working in the area," Kirkconnell wrote.

Consideration of using the park for such a site began in May 1964. Federal government officials visited the park and inspected possible locations for the camp. Within a month, the government started converting the 60-acre Central Garage Unit Area in the country's first Job Corps Center, according to Kirkconnell.

Besides building the camp, officials met with residents of Thurmont, Hagerstown, and other communities where the camp attendees might spend their off hours. They wanted to make sure that there would be a good relationship between the camp and towns.

"Thurmont merchants were wooed by an expected $200,000 in revenue from supplies, equipment and food sold to the camp for the program," Kirkconnell wrote.

Hands-on training at the Jobs Corps Training Center on Catoctin Mountain. Photo Courtesy of the Catoctin Mountain Park photo archives.

Camp officials spoke at civic meetings and invited officials and organizations out to tour the camp.

"On January 15, 1965, 85 young men between the ages of 16 and 21 arrived at Catoctin MP to inaugurate the Job Corps Program at a site "largely unimproved" since the CCC left in

1941," Kirkconnell wrote.

The Jobs Corps Center was dedicated on February 27.

The center got off to a rocky start with staffing problems and too many visiting dignitaries not only from the federal government but also foreign governments, such as Japan, Canada, British Guinea, England, Israel, the Philippines, and the Ivory Coast.

"Continual recruitment brought a total of 157 recruits into the program but 57 left before the end of June. The bleak winter contributed to homesickness; stark conditions of the camp without indoor recreation facilities and high expectations added to the general 'depressive atmosphere," Kirkconnell wrote.

Camp Director C. A. Maxey blamed the high drop-out rate on the recruits who had "temperamental and emotional problems in boys who had known little but failure," according to a *Baltimore Sun* article.

The boys had been recruited from families earning less than $3,000 a year (around $23,000 today) and had an average of a 9th-grade education. At the camp, they earned $32 a month plus $50, which was put in a bank account for them. "If they made a family allotment of $25 from the $50, the government matched it with another $25," Kirkconnell wrote.

The program included a half day of work and a half day of education in the winter. The work time increased and the education time decreased as the weather warmed up. The jobs consisted of park projects, such as building trails, picnic tables, and needed buildings. They also did work improving the Gettysburg Battlefield.

As the young men mastered basic skills, they were given more-complex work.

"A sign construction program teaching printing, mechanical drawing, hand routing, measurement skills, painting, and organizational skills produced 225 signs for Catoctin, Greenbelt, Cunningham Falls State Park and Antietam Parks in Fiscal Year 1965-1966," Kirkconnell wrote.

They also worked in the surrounding community such as building a ball field and picnic pavilion for Thurmont parks.

Students and staff at the federal job training center on Catoctin Mountain. Photo courtesy of the Library of Congress.

By 1966, things were running far more smoothly. By the end of 18 months of operation, 439 men had been recruited to the camp. And 102 had transferred out, 165 had resigned, 24 graduated, 16 went back to school or jobs, leaving 111 Corpsmen in camp at the end of June 1966, according to Kirkconnell.

By that time, it became an election year issue. Congress criticized the program and cut funding. Discipline was a problem and so were community relations.

The Job Corps Center finally closed in May 1969.

CRIME & PUNISHMENT

Bessie Darling's Murder Haunts Us Still

W hen the mail train from Baltimore stopped in Thurmont, Md., on Halloween, more than the mail was delivered. George F. Schultz, a 62-year-old employee with Maryland Health Department, left the train. Schultz hired Clarence Lidie and his taxi to give him a ride to the Valley View Hotel, which was 10 minutes away on the side of Catoctin Mountain.

As Schultz climbed into the car, Lidie noticed that he was carrying a .38-caliber revolver and mentioned on it.

"Shultz laughed and remarked that 'he didn't know what he might run into'," Edmund F. Wehrle wrote in a study about the history of Catoctin Mountain Park.

The Valley View Hotel was actually a summer boarding house, which had been run by Bessie Darling, a 48-year-old divorcee, since 1917. It was a large house built in 1907 that sat on a steep tract of land near Deerfield.

Darling, a Baltimore resident, had purchased the property from Mary E. Lent after Darling's divorce in 1917.

"She generally managed the hotel in the summer and returned to Baltimore in winter, where she used her considerable social contacts to drum up summer business for her hotel," Wehrle wrote. "Her skill at cooking and baking, as well as the scenic site helped build her a solid clientele."

In the early 20th century, people took the Western Maryland Railroad from Baltimore to Pen Mar Park to enjoy the cooler mountain temperatures and to get away from the stresses of the city. Such was the appeal of the Catoctin Mountain area as a summer retreat that visitors always needed a place to stay.

"These such boarding houses offered the women of the area a rare opportunity to operate businesses," Wehrle wrote.

Bessie Darling's house on Catoctin Mountain. Photo courtesy of Thurmontimages.com.

Schultz had known Darling since 1926. They had become so close that Schultz had even spent Christmas 1930 with

Darling's family. Newspaper accounts at the time said they were romantically linked, and he often spent weekends at the hotel while Darling was there.

Darling, who was 14 years younger than Schultz, met a lot of people, both men and women, in her work. In the summer of 1933, Schultz had become convinced that Darling was seeing Charles Wolfe, a 63-year-old man who had lost his wife a year earlier. He also lived in Foxville, much closer to the boarding house than Baltimore. (Wolfe later told the *Hagerstown Daily Mail* that he and Darling had been little more than acquaintances.)

The thought of Darling with another man made Schultz angry, and he was known for his displays of temper.

"One Thurmont resident remembered that Schultz frequently drank, and, on one occasion, assaulted Darling during an argument in front of the Lantz post office," Wehrle wrote.

While Darling forgave him that time, she was not so forgiving in this instance. Schultz and Darling got into a loud argument apparently over Wolfe, which ended when Darling left the hotel. She went to a neighbor's home to spend the night and told the neighbor that Schultz was no longer welcome in her home, according to newspaper accounts.

Darling didn't return to the hotel until Schultz left for Baltimore, and Darling didn't go back to Baltimore at the end of the tourist season. She decided that she would spend the winter in the hotel rather than have to deal with Schultz and his jealousy.

Around 7 a.m. on Halloween morning, Schultz came up to the rear entrance of the hotel as Maizie Williams, the 18-year-old maid, was coming out for firewood. Schultz demanded to see Darling. Williams said Darling was in her room and tried to close the door on the man.

Schultz forced his way inside. Williams hurried upstairs to Darling's bedroom to warn Darling with Schultz following. Williams entered the bedroom and locked the door behind her.

This didn't stop Schultz for long. He forced the lock and opened the door. Then he entered the bedroom and shot Darling who fell to the floor dead.

Bessie Darling's grave marker in Weller Cemetery in Thurmont. Photo courtesy of findagrave.com.

Schultz then calmly told Williams to make him coffee. She did, and when he finally let her leave the house to get help for Darling, he said to her, "When you come back, you'll find two of us dead."

Williams rushed out of the hotel to the nearest home with a phone. She called Frederick County Sheriff Charles Crum who drove to the hotel with a deputy around 9:30 a.m.

They entered through the basement door because Schultz had locked all of the doors and windows. When they hurried into Darling's bedroom, they found her lying dead at the foot of the bed.

They also found Schultz nearly dead from a self-inflicted

gunshot to his chest. Crum brought Dr. Morris Bireley up from Thurmont to treat Schultz, who was then taken to the hospital in Frederick, Md.

Once Schultz recovered from the wound, he was tried for murder on March 13, 1934. The prosecution called 26 witnesses in their case of first-degree murder. Schultz claimed that Darling had also had a pistol and his killing her had been an act of self-defense. The jury deliberated an hour and found him guilty of second-degree murder and Schultz was sentenced to 18 years in the Maryland State Penitentiary in Baltimore.

Wehlre recounted the story of Charles Anders who had been in the courtroom when Schultz was sentenced and, 66 years later, still remembered watching Schultz sob as the verdict was read.

The drama of the murder fed into the tabloid style journalism of the day and people followed the case with interest.

"Even today, the murder stirs an unusual amount of residual interest," Wehrle wrote.

Making Mountain Dew, White Lightning, Hooch, Moonshine

W hen the sale, production, and transportation of alcohol was banned in the United States in 1919, citizens had to choose between becoming teetotalers or criminals. Many law-abiding citizens chose the latter.

Since a person could get in trouble buying a drink, people who did it didn't talk about it. That didn't mean that it wasn't happening. Underground bars, or speakeasies, weren't advertised. People knew about them by word of mouth. You got in by knowing someone or knowing a password. Manufacturing moved to stills hidden in the woods or basements.

Moonshining (the illegal manufacture or distribution of alcohol) has been around since the Whiskey Rebellion in the 1790s. The Western Pennsylvanians who refused to pay the federal taxes on homemade liquor were the country's first moonshiners.

However, it wasn't until the Prohibition era that moonshining took off because the demand for alcohol increased. With the profits rising—a quart of moonshine could fetch $16 ($225 in today's dollars) in Hagerstown, Md.—, more and more people were willing to risk being arrested and became moonshiners, rumrunners, bootleggers.

Thurmont Moonshining

Former Catoctin Mountain Park Ranger Debra Mills explained that Catoctin Mountain was much more barren during the Prohibition era and the people who lived on it were impoverished.

"Prohibition was probably a good thing economically for people in this area," Mills said.

The remnants of a still on Catoctin Mountain. Photo courtesy of the Catoctin Mountain Park photo archives.

Having stills operating nearby gave farmers a place to sell their crops. Although corn was the most popular grain for moonshine, Elmer Black of Thurmont said in a 2015 interview that he only ever knew of rye being raised to be sold to the local moonshiners in the area.

The finished product was often shipped out of the area on the railroad in barrels labeled cornmeal, according to Mills.

It could leave other ways as well. Black recalled that his grandfather would often run moonshine right under the nose of the county sheriff and his deputies. He would get the family together to take a ride in their Studebaker and off they would go. There was an ulterior motive for the drive, though. Moonshine was hidden underneath the seats.

"My grandfather would wave 'hi' as they went by the sheriff," Black said.

Two of Black's uncles were some of the most-successful bootleggers around the Thurmont, Md., area. Even his father was known to drive moonshine out of the region to sell. One time he took, Black and his sibling along for the ride. The kids fell asleep.

"The three of us woke up and asked who lives here," Black said. "Some senator they told us. They were rolling the barrels up to the house."

They were hidden on the mountain near streams that could supply them with the water needed for the moonshine recipes. According to Black, if you follow the streams on Catoctin Mountain upriver, you can still see the remnants of stills that were destroyed.

Martin shared some of his family stories during a presentation at the Thurmont Regional Library in 2016 about moonshining.

One grandfather kept a quarter keg of moonshine in his attic, and when friends would come by with Mason jars, Martin's grandfather would tell his son to go up and get some 'shine for the friends.

At some point, Martin's grandfather moved the keg from the attic to the basement and buried it in the coal pile.

Once, revenue agents came by wanting to search the house while Martin's father was alone. The boy didn't know what to do because he couldn't get on the phone to call his parents, so he let the revenue agents in to search the house.

They started in the attic, which worried Martin's father, but the men didn't find anything. Martin's father thought he was safe and that the moonshine was no longer in the house. The revenue agents continued their search, ending up in the basement.

One of the agents saw the coal pile and wondered if moonshine might be buried in it. Martin's father, not knowing that was the case, held up the coal shovel and told the agents, "Go ahead and dig, but you've got to put it all back, or my dad will be mad."

Luckily, the agents were lazy and chose not to dig. Martin's grandfather moved the moonshine out of the house after that.

The revenue agents did eventually catch up with Martin's grandfather. According to Martin, they came in the front door of the house chasing Martin's grandfather while the man went out the back door. The federal agents chased after him.

Martin's father, a young boy at the time, chased after the men. "Dad he caught up with one revenuer and bit him on the leg and my grandfather got away," Martin said.

Moonshining in Pen Mar

Pen Mar Park, with its ideal location as a resort on the border between Maryland and Pennsylvania, became a favorite spot for bootleggers to hide their stills. Also being at Pen Mar put them close to people who wanted to relax and enjoy themselves with a drink. In 1921, an informant told police that there were 13 stills that he knew of in the vicinity of Pen Mar. The bootleggers were making a lot of money selling their product, though they didn't stay long in one place.

The *Gettysburg Compiler* reported that one informant about the bootlegging at Pen Mar saw "a bootlegger with a suitcase, placed the latter on a rock near the old Blue Mountain House path and did a land office business by handing the liquor out by the pint and half pint to people who appeared from among the bushes."

After a few minutes, he closed up shop, disappeared into the woods only to reappear in another location about half an hour or so later.

Blue Mountain House at Pen Mar was a popular tourist destination during Prohibition, which meant local bootleggers had a large customer base. Photo courtesy of the Library of Congress.

In 1925 revenuers tried to get Daniel Toms' 30-gal still in Cascade. He held them off for a short time with a shotgun, but they eventually surrounded him and caught him and his henchmen.

Smithsburg Moonshining War

Revenuers also spent plenty of time in Smithsburg, Md., combing the hills for moonshiners. They tried to pass themselves off as tourist hikers.

Smithsburg also made national headlines as having an "old-time mountain feud" between John Cline and Henry Russman involving night raiding, indiscriminate shooting, and fights. They were accused of wrecking a church, dynamiting a sawmill, killing one person, and wounding others. A 1923 article estimated that there were 500 stills between

Hagerstown and the Pennsylvania line. The interest in this fighting may have been due in part to the recent coal mine riots that had grown so violent across the country.

"They are unmolested. It would be as much as an officer's life would be worth to try and interfere. The natives are silent. They know a bullet in the dark would follow any giving of information," the *Hagerstown Mail* reported.

Moonshining in Loudoun

Although most of the known moonshiners in Loudoun County seemed to operate near the Blue Ridge Mountains, some did ply their trade around Catoctin Mountain.

"With clear springs, numerous apple and peach orchards and a sparse population in the backcountry, the Virginia Piedmont and lower Shenandoah Valley proved hospitable for bootlegging well into the 1950s. A few home distillers plied their product into the 1970s," Loudoun County historian Eugene Scheel wrote in his article, "Mountains Full of Moonshiners."

Two of the more unusual bootlegging operations were near Sterling, Va., east of Leesburg.

At the Broad Run Tollhouse, every vehicle crossing the bridge over Broad Run had to stop and pay a toll up until 1924. Many people also paid for an illegal bottle of whiskey.

Another location was in the middle of the Potomac River on Tenfoot Island. This technically placed moonshiner Earl Batt in Maryland, but the closest area with any population was in Loudoun, which is where his customer base was located.

"Whenever Batt heard that the Montgomery County sheriff might have a warrant delivered to Virginia authorities, he would dismantle the still, haul it into a powerboat and sequester the apparatus. Then he would revert to his legal occupation -- he was a stonemason, specializing in chimneys," Scheel wrote.

Broad Run Tollhouse also sold moonshine during Prohibition. Photo courtesy of Virginia Department of Historical Resources.

End of an era

Due to its unpopularity, Prohibition soon ended after the election of Franklin D. Roosevelt in 1932. Everyone went out and drank to his health.

The Mountain, the Moonshine, and the Murder

O n the evening of July 31, 1929, two cars made their way up Catoctin Mountain on Route 77, about five miles west of Thurmont, Md. The automobiles moved slowly, trying not to raise dust on the dirt road that wound through the thickly wooded ridge.

When the cars pulled off the side of the road, Frederick County Sheriff's Deputy John Hemp and compatriot Lester Hoffman climbed out. Although not a deputy, Hoffman was the only one in the group who knew his way through the forest to what Charles Lewis, a local informant, had described a week earlier as a "large liquor plant." He was talking about the Blue Blazes Still.

What happened next still remains something of a mystery, shrouded by a combination of time, folklore, and pure uncertainty. But even today, almost 90 years later, stories about the Blue Blazes and the tragic raid that put it out of business, rage on—partly because of the mystery, partly because of the bootlegging images it evokes and partly because of this fact: It marked the only time in the history of the Frederick County Sherriff's Department that a deputy died in the line of duty.

"The exact circumstances surrounding the Blue Blazes raid and the murder of (Deputy) Clyde Hauver most likely will remain a mystery and a testament to the confusing times and effects of a law with little popular support," according to

Catoctin Mountain Park: A Historic Resource Study, published by the National Park Service.

Back in the days of Prohibition, bootlegging was the invis-
ible business in Frederick County, and that business was
booming. The Catoctin Mountain, with its thick woods and
crevasses, allowed the moonshine operations to remain hidden
while still staying close to the farms that provided the grain for
the illegal liquor and the streams that provided the source of
water. According to a series of 1972 interviews conducted by
the Youth Conservation Corps, one Thurmont resident recalled
traveling to New York City during Prohibition, "where he was
stunned to learn that the high quality of Catoctin moonshine
was common knowledge in the Big Apple."

The Blue Blazes Still fermenting vats. The operation was so
huge it used the boiler from a locomotive. Photo courtesy of
Thurmontimages.com.

The stills that produced this illegal booze were large,
complex operations, often taking up acres of land and em-
ploying dozens of workers—much closer to a modern liquor

distillery than the simple contraption operated by Hawkeye and Trapper in their "M*A*S*H" tent. In 1929, *The Frederick Post* described the Blue Blazes Still as "one of the largest and best equipped in Frederick County." It used a boiler from a steam locomotive, 20 500-gallon wooden vats filled with corn mash, two condensing coils, and a cooling box. It could hold about 25,000 gallons of illegal whiskey. Former Catoctin Mountain Park Ranger Debra Mills says the still was producing moonshine so fast that if a worker took away a five-gallon bucket of alcohol and dumped it into a nearby vat, by the time he returned to the still another five gallons would be waiting to be removed.

With its liquor valued at an estimated $550,000—or $6.6 million today—it stands to reason that moonshiners were willing to take extreme measures to protect the Blue Blazes.

Even if it meant murder.

The Blue Blazes Still was reportedly the largest still found by Maryland authorities. Photo courtesy of Thurmontimages.com.

July 31, 1929

As Hemp and Hoffman began walking in the direction of the still, a man sitting on a large rock alongside the path stood up and blocked their way. According to an account in *The Frederick Post*, the exchange went like this:

"Where are yuh goin'?" the man asked.

"We want to buy some liquor," Hemp said.

"Yuh better git out of here if yuh don't want to git shot."

That was all the confirmation Hemp and Hoffman needed to know they had found the right place. So they turned around and walked back to the rest of their group. Then, joined by deputies Vernon Redmond, William Wertenbaker, William Steiner and Clyde Hauver, they all started toward the still.

Sheriff Clyde Hauver, 35,

Hauver and Redmond led the group. As they neared the still, shots rang out. Hauver fell and the deputies scattered for cover as the moonshiners, hidden by the thick underbrush, continued to shoot their weapons. The deputies returned fire. "The moonshiners retreated, but the deputies pursued," said Thurmont historian George Wireman. "It was impossible for the deputies to keep following because of the thick underbrush. They could not get close enough to shoot or even apprehend the moonshiners."

"The sheriff's forces did not immediately realize that Hauver had been mortally wounded and, thinking he had merely tripped over a root, were intent only on the capture of the moonshiners. Counting up their forces after the fusillade of firing, Hauver was missing and, returning to the scene, he was found with his head in a pool of blood, and his life was

SECRETS OF CATOCTIN MOUNTAIN

fast ebbing away," *The Frederick News* reported.

Dr. Morris Birely from Thurmont treated Hauver while waiting for an ambulance. The ambulance took Hauver to the hospital in Frederick. During the trip, Maryland State Police Officer John Taylor volunteered to give Hauver a blood transfusion, but it didn't help "Although everything possible was done for Hauver he never had a chance. When he reached the hospital he had no pulse and was nearly blood-less, so great had been the loss of blood during his time he laid in the mountain trail and during the time necessary to bring him to Frederick," reported *The Frederick Post.*

Hauver was 35 years old and the father of three young children.

The Blue Blazes Still fermenting vats, boilers, and conden-sers. Photo courtesy of Thurmontimages.com.

The Aftermath

A manhunt started for the moonshiners, and eight men were eventually arrested. But almost as quickly as the men were apprehended, so began rumors about the raid—blurring bits of fact, fiction, and folklore.

Among those jailed was Charles Lewis, the informant who, it turned out, was actually a moonshiner that some believed was merely setting up the deputies for an ambush when he led the group to Blue Blazes. He and Lester Clark were the only two people tried for murder because it was reported they were the only moonshiners armed during the raid. Their trial opened on Dec. 16, 1929, and 41 witnesses were questioned over five days, offering testimony that was both revealing and sometimes contradictory. For example, one witness from Baltimore, W.L. Poole, testified that Lewis had threatened before the raid "to get [Deputy] Redmond by fair means or foul"—spurring speculation that Hauver was not the target of the murder.

Also, the defense argued that because Hauver had been shot in the back of the head, it couldn't have been one of the moonshiners who shot him. Lawyers also pointed out that the bullet that killed Hauver didn't match any of the weapons recovered from the scene, including those of Lewis and Clark. Nonetheless, both men were convicted of murder, with Lewis receiving a life sentence and Clark serving 15 years in the state penitentiary. Maryland Gov. Theodore McKeldin commuted Lewis' life sentence in 1951 when he was 65. "He was pardoned because of ill health," Wireman says. "He wasn't out no more than two, maybe three years, before he died."

But the story lives. One rumor that persists still is that Hauver was shot by one of his own men involved in a love triangle with Hauver's wife, Eleanor. Relatives of Clyde Hauver and others point to the evidence during the trial as proof that it would be difficult for the murderers to be among the moonshiners. But if Eleanor Hauver was having an affair, no such relationship continued beyond the murder, says

James Moss, grandson of the Hauvers. He says his grand-mother never remarried after her husband's murder. "She worked hard all her life," Moss says. "I never even knew her to go out with anyone." Curiously, Moss says his grandmoth-er and mother never talked about what happened during the raid. He learned about the story only when he started talking to people on the mountain.

Despite the murder and high-profile raid, Wireman says moonshining continued on the mountain after the trial. It was only with the coming of federal agents to purchase land for the Catoctin Recreational Demonstration Area that moon-shining moved further west. In 1994, Clyde Hauver's name was added to the National Law Enforcement Officers Memo-rial in Washington D.C. He is also one of the names that will be on the Maryland Fallen Officers Memorial, which is being planned. His place in Frederick County history is secure, even if the murky stories about his death linger.

The Blue Blazes Still Today

Today, the Blue Blazes Still is gone, but the National Park Service has a 50-gallon pot still captured in a Tennessee raid on the same location. NPS uses it for presentations about moonshining in the mountains.

The NPS actually operated the still for demonstrations from 1970 to 1989. It was the first still ever to run legally on government property, according to Thurmont Historian George Wireman.

When the NPS started operating the still, the *Hagerstown Morning Herald* reported, "National Park officials hasten to assure that the whiskey is not for presidential consumption, although the pungent odor of mash undoubtedly wafts over the mountain retreat to be inhaled occasionally by VIP nostrils."

However, though the park had received permission from

the Treasury Department to manufacture whiskey, park personnel hadn't talked to state authorities about it. The *Hagerstown Morning Herald* wrote, "on the first day the still was in operation, an agent of the state's alcohol tax division appeared at the park with two deputies all set to make another raid on Blue Blazes." Since the still was on federal property, they couldn't do anything about it, though.

"I'm still known as the only park superintendent in the service who's been raided for being a moonshiner," former park superintendent Frank Mentzer told the newspaper.

The still that the National Park Service uses to stand in for the Blue Blazes Still today. Photo courtesy of the National Park Service.

The Unsolved Murder of Constable John Lloyd

J ohn R. Lloyd was finally settling down to rest from a busy day. It was near midnight on April 27, 1945. He plopped himself into a comfortable chair in the living room of his sister's house near Brunswick, Md., and turned on the radio to listen to a program.

His sister, Ella Ruble, still had a few things to do before she could rest. She was on the back porch putting milk crocks on the table.

She heard a gunshot and shattering glass.

"I ran into the kitchen and into the living room. I started to say 'John, did you hear—and then I saw him sunk back in the chair, bleeding. His face was swollen that quick," Ruble told the *Frederick Post*.

A shotgun blast through the window had hit Lloyd in the neck and right side of his head, killing him almost instantly.

Ella woke the other person who lived in the house, a boarder named George Babington. He was a brakeman for the Baltimore and Ohio Railroad. He called in the shooting to the Brunswick Police and the State Police in Frederick.

Dr. William Schnauffer also came to the house on the old Brunswick-Point of Rocks Road to examine Lloyd, but he only confirmed what Ruble already knew. Her brother was dead.

The 57-year-old Lloyd had been the constable for the Brunswick and Petersville District since 1938. As constable, he received an annual salary of $1,000 (about $15,000 in today's dollars) to serve legal papers and transport prisoners to the state prison in Baltimore. The pay supplemented the monthly pension he received from having served as a deputy.

Before becoming a constable, Lloyd had been a sheriff's deputy for many years. A railroad accident had led to both of his legs being amputated, and he got around with a cane. Lloyd was also a veteran of World War I who had seen action in France.

The police arrived quickly at Ruble's home and began investigating. Lloyd had been one of their own. The only clue the police found was the butt plate of a shotgun found near a fence. The killer had apparently lost it climbing the fence.

"The murderer evidently crept from the main Brunswick-Lander road, a short distance from the Lloyd property, up a lane to the house, waited until he had a shot that could not miss and then fired through the window pane at the constable, seated about 15 feet away," the *Frederick Post* reported.

Over the next two days, the police worked virtually around the clock, interviewing more than 40 people and following up on leads. Nothing panned out.

Since Lloyd was a constable, it was thought that he might have made an enemy of someone to whom he served papers, but he seemed well liked.

Lloyd had been very active in the community and served in a lot of organizations.

One unusual fact that came out a month after the murder was that the investigators hadn't been able to turn up any cash assets. Lloyd had no money in the house, and his savings account was virtually empty. His expenses were not excessive, so they wondered where he had been spending his money.

In July, when the trail for the killer had gone cold, Sheriff Horace Alexander convinced the Frederick County Commissioners to offer a reward for information leading to the arrest and conviction of the killer. Handbills were printed offering a $1,000 reward, and they were distributed throughout the area.

The day after the reward was announced Ruble called the police to report that three shots "had whined close to her as she walked in the year of the residence near Brunswick," according to the *Frederick Post*. While this could have been stray shots from a hunter, the fact that it happened just the day after the reward announcement couldn't be ignored.

However, the reward money was never collected. No one was ever arrested for the murder, and the leads soon went cold.

The unsolved case can still be found in the Maryland State Police's cold case files on their website.

THE WAR
BETWEEN
THE STATES

Recollections of the Civil War Near Thurmont

Sarah Six was 10 years old in 1861. Her family lived in Mechanicstown, Md. (present-day Thurmont, Md.), and Sarah grew up seeing how the Civil War affected life in town. Decades later in the early 1930s, she wrote up her recollections of the war for her son. When the writings were discovered after her death, the *Catoctin Enterprise* published them.

Her first memory associated with the Civil War was when the entire town turned out at the downtown square to see the Thurmont men march off to Frederick to be sworn in as soldiers. She wrote, "never shall I forget that morning that crowd of women trying to be brave and send off their men with smiles when their hearts were breaking."

The men seemed excited as if they were venturing off for a grand adventure. For many of them, it would be an adventure since, in the days before the Western Maryland Railroad reached Mechanicstown, they hadn't ever ventured far from town in their lives.

In the years to come, the wives and mothers of Mechanicstown would live in a state of anxiety wondering what had become of the husbands and children. News about the war did not arrive often. There was no daily newspaper, and mail came only three times a week. The telegraph had not been installed in town, and the telephone did not exist.

"News traveled slowly and when there was a battle on,

many days would elapse before any report of it reached our town," Sarah wrote.

In support of their Union soldiers, the women of Mechanicstown would often gather at St. John's Lutheran Church to bag up old linen that would be sent off to Union hospitals to be turned into bandages. Sarah and other children would do their part by gathering wild cotton that was also sent to the hospitals.

One night around midnight in 1862, the Six family was awakened by a barking dog. Then they heard Henry Foreman, the neighbor's son, calling, "Get up, Mr. Six! The rebels are coming."

The family got dressed and turned out into the street along with the rest of the town. In the dark of night, they watched army ambulances come through the town with wounded that they were transporting to safety in Pennsylvania. They also came with news that the rebels had crossed the Potomac River.

Most likely this would have been early in the morning of September 5. After Gen. Robert E. Lee's victory at the Second Battle of Bull Run at the end of August, Lee moved his army into Maryland with the intention of securing a victory in the North. He wanted to keep his army on the offensive and influence the fall elections in the North so that congressmen and senators willing to recognize the Confederate States of America might be elected. Also, Lee needed supplies for his army that the South was running out of.

As the army had approached Frederick, citizens, military, and patients from the United States Military Hospital fled the city.

As the Union ambulances moved through Mechanicstown, drivers and patients requested food and coffee. It was provided as much as the citizens could manage, but Sarah noted that because the town had no bakeries, many homes went without bread for breakfast that day.

Some of the residents in a town packed up and headed north with the army. Others hunkered down and hid valuables, livestock, and food.

"Mother had valuables packed and ready to flee into the mountain I had few treasures but two of them were in my pocket—a small silk union flag and my treasured china doll," Sarah wrote.

The Confederate army did not continue north from Frederick. They turned west and would go on to fight the Battle of South Mountain and the Battle of Antietam before retreated south back across the Potomac.

The Six family lived in a state of uncertainty. They knew very little of their friends and family who had marched off to war. They didn't fear an invasion so much as worried about losing what they had to Confederate scavengers.

Word had spread through the region that Confederate soldiers were taking horses and cattle when they found them. If they paid, they paid in Confederate scrip. Sarah's father, William Six, was so worried about losing his stock that he took his two horses north to Wrightsville, Pa.

One night while William was away, Sarah was spending the night with her friend Mollie Foreman. The young girls were sleeping in the back of the house when they heard something that awakened them. They realized that it was the steady tramp of horses' hooves.

They crept downstairs, unlocked the front door and stepped out onto the front porch. From an upstairs window, someone whispered hoarsely, "Go in and shut that door!"

"I can tell you, we went up those stairs quietly but faster than we had gone down, for when we realized we were down there alone and in inky darkness, we felt as if a rebel was after us for sure and we were scolded good and proper," Sarah wrote.

All they had been able to see were the shifting shapes of horsemen moving in the night. In the morning, she found out that the men had been suspected Confederate soldiers.

While the town had hidden from the Confederates, they were overjoyed when Union soldiers came to town.

"Everyone (except southern sympathizers) came on the streets and with waving flags, gave them a welcome for they were usually close on the heels of a reported invasion, which made them doubly welcome," Sarah wrote.

Another night, the town was once again awakened by troops riding through town. This group stopped in front of the Six house when they saw a light shining in a second-floor window. They called up to the person in the lighted room.

William wouldn't answer them, but Sarah's mother walked to the window and called out, "What do you want?"

"Where does George Johnson live?" one of the men replied.

"Who are you?"

"We are Union men. We are going to Chimney Rock to display signals. We were told Mr. Johnson would feed our horses and point the way to the mountain."

"How do I know that you are Union men?"

The soldier rode up close to the house and into the light. "See the uniform?" the soldier asked.

She did, but she still doubted. The soldier finally talked her into telling him where Johnson lived. He was home. He fed the soldiers' horses and then led the men up Catoctin Mountain in the dark. Eventually, those people who were still awake did see signals on the mountain.

Since there were no street lights, children stayed close to home as night began to fall. They would sit on their porches and sing Union songs.

Mechanicstown was 18 miles from Gettysburg, Pa., but it might as well have been hundreds of miles, according to Sarah. She knew the name of the town and that it had a college in it, but that was all. Sarah wrote that the road to Gettysburg was in bad shape and full of stones that it was sarcastically nicknamed "featherbed."

She remembers seeing the soldiers marching to Gettysburg. "The weather was cloudy with rain and very sultry," Sarah wrote. "It hurts me even now as I can see those poor men on that forced march in heavy wool uniforms, not allowed to stop for a drink but some would scoop up a hand full from the gutter alongside the street."

They heard nothing of the battle until they started seeing weary soldiers marching south.

She also remembered the solemn tolling of the church bells after news of President Abraham Lincoln's assassination was announced.

Sad memories for a child to have.

Catoctin Mountain's
Path to Freedom

A fter 15 years of abuse, Peyton Lucas had finally
found a life that he enjoyed. He had apprenticed
with a blacksmith for five years, and by 1841, he
had been working as a journeyman for six years.

True, he was still a slave, and his wages went to his
owner, but as Lucas wrote in *North-Side View of Slavery*, a
collection of first-person accounts of slaves who escaped to
freedom that was published in 1856, "I enjoyed life then very
well, and had many privileges: nor did I run away for either
fear of my master, of the man I lived with, nor in
consequence of ill treatment."

It hadn't always been that way. He had been born into
slavery in 1815 in Leesburg, Va. His owner was a Baptist
minister.

He did not have to endure too much of the horrors of
slavery until he reached the age of 12 or 13. He typically only had a coarse crocus shirt that was uncomfortable to wear.
"Many a time have I taken it by the two ends, and pulled it
round a post to break down the sticks," he wrote.

Crocus was a type of coarse, homespun cloth often worn
by slaves. It made on the East Coast in the 18th and 19th centuries. "The stuff is obsolete and the name is forgotten save
in a folk-saying which lingers in Virginia—'as coarse as crocus,'" Alice Morse Earle wrote in his article "Hand Waving."

When Lucas hit his teen years, he was seen as someone

who should be useful around the house or barnyard. If his performance was disappointing, the master let him know it.

"My master never sent me to school, not gave me any instruction from the Bible, excepting one passage of Scripture which he used to quote to me, -- 'He that knoweth his master's will, and doeth it not, she be beaten with many stripes,'" Lucas wrote.

This usually happened right before he was taken into the barnyard and beaten with rawhide stripes.

As bad as Lucas's master was, his mistress was probably worse. She often beat Lucas over the head with a dairy key "as big as a child's fist." Lucas said that she would find a reason to complain about his work. The master would then kick him and haul him out to the barnyard to be whipped.

The master would tell him, "now, you know better than to aggravate your mistress as you do, for you've often heard me read, 'He that knoweth,' etc.," Lucas wrote.

Lucas found a way to shorten his beatings. He screamed like he was being murdered. The master didn't like all of the attention that drew his way and would stop.

One day, Lucas's brother was playing in the yard with another slave boy. They had a dog that would protect Lucas's brother if he called "Help, Bull." The brother demonstrated, and the dog nipped the other slave boy. The boy was either hurt more than he appeared or wanted to get back at Lucas's brother. Either way, he told the overseer who told the master what had happened.

The master had the boy tied to a post and gave him 25 lashes with the whip. He handed the whip to the overseer and told him, "Brother, take your satisfaction out of the dog, (meaning my brother,) and then let him down."

The master then mounted his horse and went to preach a sermon.

That evening, Lucas's brother stole one of the master's horses and rode off. He was never caught, but the master did get the horse back from someplace in Baltimore.

The master also sold Lucas's other brother, one of his sisters, and two of his sister's children to a master in Georgia.

It's not known whether Lucas ever saw any of them again.

When Lucas turned 15, he was hired out to a local blacksmith. He worked five years as an apprentice learning the skills and then became a journeyman who could be paid for his work.

Although Lucas enjoyed life with the blacksmith, he was still a slave. One of his sisters worked in the blacksmith's house, and she overheard the blacksmith talking to a stranger about buying Lucas.

Escape

When Lucas realized that his life might soon take a turn for the worse, he followed his brother's example and planned his escape. Within a week, he and two other slaves headed north, most likely following the Carolina Road, which was a route along the Underground Railroad.

Once he escaped, Peyton Lucas decided to change his name to Charles Bentley.

Bentley and his two companions pushed themselves hard that first night and made it as far as the southern shore of the Potomac River.

They hid for the day, and the next night, they tied their provisions on their backs and swam and waded across the river. "At last we reached the opposite bank in Maryland: we merely stopped to pour the water out of our boots, and then hid in the bushes," Lucas wrote.

They then spent 10 days apparently wandering around the

eastern slope of Catoctin Mountain, lost, suffering from hunger, and not realizing they were in a relatively safe zone.

Cooling Springs Farm

Cooling Springs Farm is just north of the Potomac River in Frederick County. According to the farm's website, "The family's passed-down oral tradition is that freedom seekers escaping slavery were sheltered by the Michael family in the farm's spring house."

This is not conclusive documentary proof, but it is an oral tradition passed down through seven generations. This means that the story would have originated at the time the Underground Railroad was in operation and was not created sometime after the war.

Ezra and Henry Michael were brothers who owned Cooling Springs Farm and an adjoining farm between Point of Rocks, Md., and Doubs, Md. The brothers' in-laws also owned farms adjoining the Michaels brothers. This created a three-mile-long piece of land owned by anti-slavery families that ran from the Potomac River to some of Frederick County's black-founded villages (Doubs, Pleasant View, Hall Town, and Adamstown).

Ezra and his wife, Margaret, lived on Cooling Springs Farm during the mid-19th century. "Margaret Michael came from the abolitionist Dudderar family of Urbana, Frederick County, Maryland, and it appears to have been she who was the instigator of Michael family involvement in the Underground Railroad. Ezra Michael was a judge who, the family likes to say, upheld the law of man by day and followed a higher law by night in aiding freedom seekers," according to the farm website.

Escaping slaves who made it across the river could feel relatively safe traveling through the Michaels' family properties. If they wished, they could blend in among free blacks in the villages or the Michaels would help them continue their journey on an actual railroad. In this case, it was the Baltimore and Ohio Railroad that ran through the property. According to the family, the springhouse, which is located only a short distance from the railroad tracks was the safe house for the escaped slaves.

Lost on the Underground Railroad

As for Bentley and his companions, they were near safety but afraid to approach it. They could hear the people nearby from their hiding places, but they didn't dare take a chance of asking for help.

"For three days, we had neither food nor drink, excepting green corn," Bentley wrote. "We sucked the juice for drink, and the corn itself was our only food. The effect of this was to weaken us very much."

One night they broke into a springhouse to try and get milk, but dogs started barking, and they ran off before anyone came to investigate.

Out of desperation, they finally approached a lime kiln worker to ask for directions. They made up a story about being finished harvesting and looking for work. The man didn't believe the lie. Bentley drew his pistol, and the others pulled knives. The man wasn't trying to capture them, though. Bentley wrote, "he proved to be the best friend we had ever had."

The worker told them they were only a day's walk away from the Mason-Dixon Line and that once they crossed it, they would be among the Dutch. He gave them directions to a Dutchman's house and told them to travel during the day but keep to the woods.

The runaways reached the house the next morning and were welcomed. The family fed them.

"We ate all they had in the house, -- I ate till I was ashamed," Bentley wrote.

They were warned to avoid Shippensburg because six escaped slaves had been captured there recently and returned to their masters. The Dutch family home was actually a station on the Underground Railroad in Pennsylvania. Now in safe hands, the runaways were sent on with directions to the next station.

The journey from Leesburg to Cooling Springs Farms usually took about three days, according to Scheel. It then took another day or two to reach the safety of Pennsylvania. Bentley and his fellow runaways took nearly two weeks to travel the same distance.

Bentley made it to Geneva, N. Y., where he worked and started his family. However, when Congress passed the Fugitive Slave Act in 1850, Bentley's friends urged him to move to Canada.

The law was a compromise between Southern and Northern interests. However, it required that all escaped slaves were, upon capture, to be returned to their masters and that officials and citizens of free states had to cooperate with this law.

Lucas eventually married and had children. His family settled in Toronto, Canada, in 1850 according to a brochure called "Black Victorian Life" developed by the City of Toronto Culture Division. Lucas set up a successful blacksmith trade in the city, "that lead one observor (sic) to describe him as 'at the head of his trade,'" according to the brochure. The business, which was located on Centre Street in the city, continued in the 1860s.

Scheel wrote that more than 1,000 slaves made their trek to freedom Loudoun and Frederick counties.

The Occupation of Emmitsburg

M other Ann Simeon of the Daughters of Charity shared an apartment with her secretary Sister Marie Louise Caulfield at St. Joseph College in Emmitsburg, Md. On Saturday night, June 27, 1863, Mother Ann Simeon had already turned in, but Sister Marie Louise was still awake when she heard unfamiliar sounds outside the building. As the noises drew closer, she made out the neighing of horses among them.

She rose from her bed and looked outside. She saw lights flashing on and off on a hill near the end of the toll gate that was nearby. With the rumors of approaching armies that had been circulating throughout the town, Sister Marie Louise realized that it was no longer a rumor.

The soldiers did not approach the Central House that evening. Instead, they found the overseer, Joseph Brawner, who lived with his wife in a little house between the academy and the toll gate. The soldiers asked Brawner's permission to camp on the fields that first night.

On Sunday, Brawner was given a memo that entitled him to be paid for 16,000 pounds of hay that the arriving Army of the Potomac had consumed on the farm.

General Philippe Regis de Trobriand was a French aristocrat who also commanded the Third Brigade of the First Division of the Third Corps. He wrote about his impressions of St. Joseph's the following morning in *Four Years with the Army of the Potomac* saying, "I leave it to you to guess if the good sisters were not excited, on seeing the guns moving along under their windows and the regiments, bristling with bayonets, spreading out through their orchards. Nothing like it had ever troubled the calm of this holy retreat. When I arrived at a gallop in front of the principal door, the doorkeeper, who had ventured a few steps outside, completely lost her head. In her fright, she came near being trampled under foot by the horses of my staff, which she must have taken for the horses of the Apocalypse, -- if, indeed, there are any horse in the Apocalypse, of which I am not sure."

St. Joseph College in Emmitsburg during the Civil War. Photo courtesy of the Library of Congress.

The general met Mother Ann Simeon in her parlor and was impressed by her calm and dignity, particularly in the face of the reception he had received earlier. He noted that Mother Ann Simeon grasped the situation and did not object when de Trobriand asked to go to the cupola to observe the surrounding land.

With so many troops encamped on the grounds of their school and Central House, the sisters began to worry that a battle might be fought on their doorsteps.

General Oliver Howard with his staff stayed in the Vincentian residence where Father Francis Burlando lived in

Emmitsburg. General Carl Schurz and his officers remained in the White House.

To safeguard the property and Sisters at Emmitsburg, the Union generals stationed guards at various points. "Here and there they were dotted standing on guard two hours, fagged out with fatigue, and hungry as wolves," Sister Mary Louise wrote about the guards.

The sisters quickly took on the charitable duty of feeding the soldiers. The soldiers began asking the sisters for food the day after they arrived. "The poor fellows looked half-starved,--lank as herrings and barefoot," Sister Mary Jane Stokes wrote after the war in a letter to Burlando.

The sisters spent their day slicing meat, buttering bread, and filling canteens with coffee or milk.

On June 29, D. Agnew, justice of the peace in Emmitsburg, signed a statement of damages the sisters used to get paid for some of the food they provided the army. Though the list did not include the bread and cold meats given the soldiers, it did list: 109 cord wood of fuel at $2.50 a cord, 13.5 tons of hay at $9 a ton and 120 bushels of rye at a dollar a bushel.

Sister Mary Jane was the sister in charge of the farm. She saw soldiers who were hungry and could not deny them a meal. So the sisters gave freely of what they had, although it quickly diminished their own supplies since feeding an army required much more than feeding a couple hundred sisters and students. As the sisters continued to liberally supply all of the soldiers who came asking for food, she realized that the day's bread was quickly disappearing. She went to the bakehouse to see if there would be any bread left for the sisters and was surprised to find that the day's baking hadn't been touched. She wrote later, "After supper, I belonged to the kitchen Sisters, I went to Mother Ann Simeon and told her I didn't know what the Sisters would do for breakfast the next morning, for they would have no bread. Then I went to see, and there was the baking of the day was there. I did not see it *multiply, but I did see it there!*"

While the sisters took on the job of feeding the soldiers, Fathers Burlando and Gandolfo and another priest from Emmitsburg heard confessions from the Catholic soldiers. "The fathers remained as long as there was a soldier to be heard and invested with a pair of scapulars. Never did we witness such satisfaction as to see those poor men express their hope and confidence in the Mother of God that she would save their souls any way, even if they should fall in the terrible battle that they were facing," Sister Camilla O'Keefe wrote after the war.

Mother Ann Simeon also took care to separate her female students and sisters from the soldiers. The doors to the seminary building were kept locked at all times. On one occasion, two sisters left on an errand, and when they returned, they found themselves locked out of the building.

Early on June 30, 1863, the order was given to strike camp. "In fifteen minutes, it was done and St. Joseph's Valley relapsed into quiet." Sister Camilla wrote, "Not a vestige of the great Army was to be seen…Glad we were to get rid of them."

While the Daughters of Charity were committed to showing no favoritism in their treatment of the soldiers, the same didn't hold true for the girls who boarded at the academy. Many of them were from Confederate states and were trapped in a country at war with their home states. As the soldiers prepared to leave, one girl climbed into the cupola and signaled to Confederate scouts where the Union troops were and that they were leaving, according to Mary Bernard McEntee in *The Valley*.

It wasn't long after the Union Army had headed north out of Emmitsburg when the Confederate Army appeared on the horizon. Though a much smaller army, estimated at only

10,000 men, the soldiers generated much more excitement in the town and at St. Joseph's Academy.

So quick was the switch between the armies during the night that Father Gandolfo did not realize control of the town had changed hands. The next morning, Father Gandolfo came out to St. Joseph's early to say Mass and was halted by Confederate pickets.

Not recognizing the soldiers as Confederate and not knowing the Union Army had moved out, Father Gandolfo said, "But I am going to say Mass at St. Joseph's. We have General Howard at our house."

Though admitting he was housing a Union general didn't help his case, things managed to get straightened out, and he was allowed to continue.

The following morning, the 107th Regiment, Pennsylvania Volunteers, Second Division First Corps marched toward Emmitsburg on their way to Gettysburg. As they passed by St. Joseph's Academy, they were greeted by the sight of a long line of girls and Daughters of Charity along the side of the road.

At a word from the sister in charge, the females dropped to their knees and lifted their faces to the sky. They then began praying for the spiritual and physical safety of the soldiers marching to battle.

The scene touched the men who stopped, removed their caps and bowed their heads until the women had finished the prayer.

The soldiers then continued their march.

Not long after, the calm of the day was shattered by the booming of distant cannon. Father Burlando wrote later, "While the cannon's roar announced the vengeance of God on the iniquities of man, our Sisters were at prayer in the Chapel imploring mercy for all."

The Battle of Gettysburg had begun.

The Great Calico Raid

B
y 1864, the tides of war had shifted to favor the Union. However, the rebels weren't beaten yet. Although Union Gen. Ulysses Grant had Confederate Gen. Robert E. Lee was pinned down around Richmond and Petersburg, Lee sent Maj. Gen. Jubal Early's Second Corps to help defend the Shenandoah Valley.

On June 18, he defeated Union Maj. Gen. David Hunter at Lynchburg. This left him with a clear path to the Potomac River. He began moving his 20,000 men north.

Col. John Mosby and his Confederate Rangers began raiding Maryland communities along the river to screen Early's advance.

"Although he never admitted it, Mosby clearly sought to ride Early's coat tails in an attempt to enhance his reputation and his transformation into a member of Virginia's elite," Arnold M. Pavlovsky wrote in In *Pursuit of a Phantom: John Singleton Mosby's Civil War.*

Rangers were smaller units that cooperated with the Confederate Army but operated independently, moving more quickly in smaller companies.

Mosby's Rangers left Upperville, Va., on July 3. It was a 100-plus degree day, and the ground was dry, which made it a dusty, unpleasant ride to Bloomfield, Va., for the 250 Rangers and their four howitzers.

During their ride north, Mosby had his men spread a disinformation campaign. Northern Loudoun County was pro-Union, so Mosby instructed his men to answer any questions about who they were and what they were doing to say that they were an advance guard of Longstreet's Corps.

They arrived at the Potomac River the next day. Scouts reported that Union soldiers were in Point of Rocks and a picket was on Patton Island in the river. Mosby examined the situation himself and discovered that the Union soldiers were members of the Loudoun Rangers, a Union Ranger unit formed in Loudoun County. They were manning a small earthwork overlooking the river.

Col. John S. Mosby

Mosby had one of the cannon fire on the island. He wrote later, "As this was the first occasion on which I had used artillery, the magnitude of the invasion was greatly exaggerated by the fears of the enemy, and panic ... spread through their territory."

The cannon fire was aided by two dozen sharpshooters under the command of Lt. Albert Wren. They provided cover fire as the Rangers began swimming their horses across the river.

Confederate Gen. Thomas "Stonewall" Jackson had burned the bridge on June 9, 1861, to try and keep Union troops from crossing into Loudoun County.

Under fire, and facing the approaching Rangers, the Union soldiers fled the village heading toward Frederick.

The Leesburg Bridge that passed over the Potomac River at Point of Rocks. Scanned from *Harpers Weekly*.

Once the Rangers reached the Maryland shore, they faced another obstacle. They still had to get their men and horses across the six-foot-deep C&O Canal. A permanent bridge spanned the canal near lock 28, but the Union soldiers had removed the planks from it. Mosby's men had to rip boards from an old warehouse to make temporary flooring for the bridge so the men could cross into town.

"Most of the men went into the dry-goods business, and soon four regular shops and one sutler's establishment were emptied of their contents," Maj. John Scott of the Rangers wrote in his memoir.

One of the shopkeepers, Louis Meems, told Mosby that he was a southerner, his goods were returned.

The men also took cigars, food, and liquor from a canal boat that had the misfortune of being near Point of Rocks at the wrong time. Telegraph wires were cut and logs laid across the railroad tracks.

When a train approached the village from Harpers Ferry, the howitzers began shelling it. The engineer managed to get the train in reverse and escape. However, the Rangers knew the Union army would soon know of the situation in town.

The men burned the Union camps and then retreated across the river. "Finally having filled up their sacks with loot, the Rangers swam their horses across the river and returned to Virginia. Some of the men were wearing bonnets and carrying large bolts of cloth," Pavlovsky wrote.

They traveled down the Carolina Road until they found a place to make camp. Maj. Scott wrote, "As they passed along the road, some arrayed in crinoline, some wearing bonnets, and all disguised with some incongruous and fantastic article of apparel, they looked like a company of masqueraders."

This led to the skirmish being called "The Great Calico Raid."

That evening, the Rangers celebrated by drinking confiscated whiskey and eating pound cake that had been found in a Union officer's tent, according to Pavlovsky.

The next day, Mosby sent three wagonloads of the captured goods along with 100 men to Fauquier County.

LIFE ON CATOCTIN MOUNTAIN

The Legend of Catoctin Furnace

"When the legend becomes fact, print the legend." That's what a newspaper editor tells James Stewart's character in *The Man Who Shot Liberty Valence*. It's also what has happened to the story of Catoctin Furnace over the centuries.

For more than 125 years, Isabella, Deborah, and an unnamed stack; the three furnaces of Catoctin Furnace; produced hundreds of tons of pig iron annually that helped build the United States before there was a United States.

The furnace's real history is illustrative of industry in America. It even has its brush with fame because one of the early partners in the venture was Thomas Johnson, the first governor of Maryland. In later years, it has had U.S. Presidents beginning with Herbert Hoover camp or stay nearby.

That's a proud history, a fine history, but the legends…

The legends lift the Catoctin Furnace from one of many iron-smelting furnaces in early Maryland to a linchpin of American history.

Some believe iron from Catoctin Furnace defended America with cannonballs for the Continental Army, furthered American ingenuity with parts for James Rumsey's steamboat engine, and changed naval warfare with the iron plates that protected the U.S.S. Monitor during the Civil War.

The truth, however, is somewhat different.

Ready Materials

Despite a failed furnace on the west side of the Catoctin

Mountains, the area south of Thurmont, Md., was a natural site for an iron furnace. The furnace in Washington County failed because the ore was not good quality. That wasn't the case with the Catoctin Furnace operation. The iron ore for the furnaces came from three sites on the property. Two ore banks were located behind the furnace. The third site was a mile north and the largest of the three, measuring 800 feet by 2,000 feet.

Catoctin Furnace in Thurmont. Photo courtesy of Thurmontimages.com

When the ore was mined, first by hand and later by steam shovels, the iron ore was mixed with clay. It took seven tons of clay to produce one ton of ore. That one ton of iron was a good grade, though. It was 40 percent hydrous ferric oxide, limonite.

Not only was the iron ore good quality, but all of the needed materials to turn that ore into pig iron were also there.

The Catoctin Mountains provided the timber required for charcoal and basins for stream systems. Charcoal provided the heat for the whole process. Estimates are that the blast furnace used 800 bushels of charcoal a day. This required 5,000 to 6,000 cords of wood each year or an acre of 20- to 25-year-old hardwood each day. Water was used to wash the clay from the ore and drive the water wheel, which operated the furnace bellows. Limestone from nearby quarries was added to the ore to serve as a flux to remove impurities.

With an abundance of needed resources, it was only a matter of time before someone discovered all the ingredients for a successful mining operation. That someone was the Johnson Brothers and the time was 1774.

Catoctin Furnace in Thurmont. Photo courtesy of Thurmon-timages.com

Smelting iron

The business of Catoctin Furnace was producing iron, and the furnaces and workers did that for more than 125 years.

The furnaces produced pig iron in 80-100 pound bars that

were five to six feet long and six inches around. The brown hematite ore was initially mined from the ground by pick and shovel. The ore was washed to remove the clay and then the clean ore was hauled by mule to the top of the furnace where it was dumped in a 12-foot opening and melted into pig iron.

The stone and brick furnaces were at least 32 feet tall and somewhat smaller at the base. "If the height was greater, the weight of the iron ore and limestone tended to crush the lower layers of charcoal, clogging the furnace," Frank Mentzer wrote in a series of articles about the history of Catoctin Furnace. The sides tapered inward. The interiors of the furnaces were lined with fire bricks and a rubble chamber between the brick and the exterior walls. The inner chamber was shaped like a soda bottle, open at the top. A few feet from the bottom was an air blast nozzle. Air was blown into the furnace by a bellows worked by a water wheel.

To produce one ton of iron, you needed 1¾ tons of ore, ¾ ton of charcoal, ¼ ton of limestone and 4 tons of air.

Before the furnace was started, all of the materials had to be placed in the furnace. The first layer was charcoal, then a layer of limestone and then a layer of iron ore. Additional layers in that order could be laid down until the furnace was filled to the top.

The fire was then started. Originally, it was kept burning by a natural draft. Later forced air was used. Heating the furnace started a number of chemical reactions in the materials.

"Charcoal burns with a greater heat than wood, and when this heat reached 2800 degrees F the iron in the ore began to melt and trickle down to the hearth. In addition to providing the necessary heat to melt the iron, the burning coal gave off carbon as a gas which combined with oxygen from the air to form carbon monoxide. As this gas moved upward through the iron oxide, it combined with the oxygen in the ore to form carbon dioxide, freeing the iron. As the melted iron trickled down to the hearth it dissolved a small amount of the carbon," according to Mentzer.

By adding limestone to the burn mix, impurities melted at a lower temperature than the iron. The limestone would then combine with the impurities to form slag, a waste material.

"As the contents would burn and the iron melt and settle to the bottom, more charcoal or coke, limestone and iron ore would be added. This purpose continued until there was sufficient melted iron to draw off or be cast," Fern Rice wrote in *Catoctin Furnace*.

At the bottom of the furnace was a channel. As the iron flowed to the bottom of the channel, a worker would use a long hook and open a clay valve at the bottom of the furnace.

"When the iron was cast it would flow into channels or shallow troughs previously made ready by furrowing out long lines in the ground. These channels were sprinkled with sand to prevent the iron from adhering to the ground. The product obtained from the furnace was called pig iron. Some people say it was called pig iron because as the molten metal flowed along the main channel into a series of small sand molds, it made a noise which suggested pigs sucking a sow. Since the channels were marked off into sections approximately two feet long, it was easy to break the iron into 'pigs' and carry them when sufficiently cooled. The 'pigs' were stacked in rows like cordwood and were then ready for shipment," Rice wrote.

If the iron were to be used for hollow ware, it would be caught in a ladle as it came out of the bottom of the furnace and poured into the mold.

Once the pig iron cooled, it could be broken into transportable bars for use in casting pots, pans, kettles, stoves, tools, farm implements, shot or shells. Iron from the furnace was also cast as a popular pot-belly stove called a "Catoctin Stove."

The length of time the furnace burned was called a "blast." Once the furnace was lighted, it was kept burning until the stocks of charcoal, iron ore and limestone were used up or until freezing winter weather halted the waterwheel that powered the bellows to the furnace.

Birth of a Nation, Birth of a Company

The land containing Catoctin Furnace was part of a 7,715-acre "Mountain Tract" obtained by Leonard Calvert and Thomas Johnson in 1768, but in 1774, Calvert transferred his interest to Thomas' other brothers, James, Baker and Roger and the brothers formed James Johnson and Company with the intention of building an iron-smelting operation.

"Catoctin furnace, situated about twelve miles northwest of Fredericktown, and within a mile of the present furnacestack, 'was built in the year 1774, by James Johnson and Company and was carried on successfully until the year 1787'; in which year, the same company erected the present furnace 'about three-fourth of a mile further up Little Hunting Creek, and nearer the ore banks,'" J. H. Alexander wrote in *Report on the Manufacture of Iron Addressed to the Governor of Maryland*.

This makes the first furnace at Catoctin Furnace the 16th in Maryland, according to the *Maryland Geological Survey*. It was 32 feet high and surrounded by other needed equipment and machinery such as a water wheel, mill pond, and races, a coal house to store charcoal, the bridge and bridge house to charge the stack and a cast house. "The furnace operation also needed homes for its workmen, a store to supply their needs, barns, and stables for the furnace stack, and a home for the ironmaster and his family. The 28 by 36 foot stone Manor House is believed to have been built at this time," for Park Superintendent Frank Mentzer wrote in a series of articles about the history of Catoctin Furnace for the *Frederick News*.

This also became the beginnings of the community of Catoctin Furnace. The various jobs associated with running the furnace required men to do them. Miners dug the iron from the ground. Lumberers felled the trees and colliers prepared the charcoal from them. Fillers charged the furnace. Founders smelted the iron and cast it. And all of these people made their homes near the furnace.

The coal-fueled furnace went operational in the fall of 1775 in the midst of the Revolutionary War, which set the scene for the formation of the first significant legend surrounding the furnace.

Cannonballs for the Army

In the midst of its war for independence, the American government, such as it was, sought material to carry on the war. In 1776, "The Council of Safety wrote Colonel James Johnson in mid-July, inquiring as to his ability to supply 60 cannons, 40 swivels (smaller than regular cannon and mounted to swing on a pivot), and 200 iron pots. A week later, and without waiting for an answer to their first letter, they increased their 'order' to 175 cannon," Mentzer wrote.

Thomas Johnson replied saying that his company could supply about 60 kettles and Dutch ovens with the expectation that more could be made within a short time. The committee wasn't interested in them.

As for the cannon, Johnson was doubtful of his ability to make them at Catoctin Furnace. He wrote the council, "We shall also attempt to cast such guns as are wanted but cannot contract for them in all Events because the metal may not suit, though we have every Reason to expect it will. If we succeed in making good Gun the Public may have them del'd at Baltimore at 40 L a Ton the Guns being proved at the works at the public Expense, that swivels at their common price, but I should be glad if you would ascertain the length & other Descriptions as the make of cannon carrying the same shot vary very much. If any Body also will contract for a Certainty, I wish he should be preferred even at a greater price," according to *A History of American Manufactures 1608 to 1860.*

Casting cannon required a specialized knowledge that the ironmasters at Catoctin Furnace didn't have according to Mentzer. The molds were made of a special mix of sand and clay and using a similar technique as used for casting bells. The molds were then lowered into pits near the mouth of the furnace and earth was carefully packed around them. "Instead of filling the mold from the top, which could trap air and cause defects, a vertical runner was made to fill from the bottom, forcing the air out of the top," Mentzer wrote.

There is no record of cannon being successfully cast at Catoctin Furnace, but the ammunition for the cannon the Continental Army did have…now, that's a different story.

"Henry Knox, Washington's Colonel Commandant of Artillery, noted in his 1781 inventory that they had on hand 950 ten-inch shells cast at Catoctin Furnace," Mentzer wrote.

While the dates would have allowed those shells to be used in the decisive Battle of Yorktown as a legend and the Maryland State Road Commission sign at the park notes, the only reference to this event is unverified letters the Johnson Brothers wrote.

Rumsey's Steamboat

Following the Revolutionary War, Catoctin Furnace's next venture into legend related to James Rumsey's steamboat. Rumsey was a Maryland inventor who built a steam-powered water-jet that propelled a boat upstream on the Potomac River.

Baker Johnson's great-great-granddaughter told the Columbia Historical Society in 1913 that Thomas Johnson had been with Washington to witness the steamboat on March 14, 1786, and that some of the machinery was manufactured at Catoctin Furnace.

"Afterwards the machinery was taken back to Catoctin and for many years the cylinder, four inches in diameter, stood three feet above ground as a boundary between the Catoctin Furnace property and the land of William Johnson," according to *Records of the Columbia Historical Society.*

Though this shaft was never found, *The Baltimore Sun* noted in a 1925 article, "A large iron shaft, which marks as a cornerstone a street in Frederick, was cast for one of Rumsey's boats at Governor Johnson's forge." This shaft is encased in cement at the corner of West Patrick Street and Maxwell Avenue. It is said to be a marker on the National Road, but it is unlike most markers on the road, which lends credence to the idea that it could be a shaft from Rumsey's steamboat.

However, the 1936 federal government report on the historical features of Cunningham Falls State Park looked at the historical claims of Catoctin Furnace and found, "we have proof that the boiler, pumps, and pipes were made in Baltimore and that other parts were made at Antietam Iron Works." Mentzer also wrote that Catoctin Furnace wasn't able to manufacture the thin-walled cylinders that the Rumsey needed and, instead, copper cylinders were made for him in Frederick Town.

Lacking hard evidence, this is one of the historical claims about the furnace that remains in doubt.

The Johnson Brothers dissolved their partnership in 1793

and Thomas and Baker Johnson took control of the furnace. They ran it until 1803. Baker then bought out his brother and took sole control of the furnace. He, in turn, rented the property to Benjamin Blackford for 10 years at $1,100 (about $13,000 in today's dollars), according to Frederick County land records.

However, after Baker Johnson's death in 1811, the property was sold to Willoughby and Thomas Mayberry. They paid 12,500 pounds for the land. Their partnership was later dissolved, and Willoughby took over the operation until 1820.

During their tenure, Willoughby and Mayberry started producing ten-plate stoves that could be used for cooking as well as heating. "Thus the thrifty Germans of the Monocacy Valley were among the first people of America to have the advantages of this more efficient method of heating," Mentzer wrote.

John Brien bought the furnace and made extensive improvements to the operation. During his ownership, the 32-foot high furnace produced 12-18 tons of pig iron a week, which slaves floated down the Monocacy to the markets, according to the *Maryland Geological Survey*.

Brien's wife, Harriet, died in 1827. He built a small stone chapel for her near the furnace operations. Harriet Chapel was consecrated in 1833 and continues to serve the Episcopal community.

Peregrine Fitzhugh became the next owner in 1843. He discontinued making hollow ware goods and instead resumed shipping the pig iron downriver. He built a new charcoal furnace that was named Isabella. This is the furnace that still remains on the site of Catoctin Furnace. Isabella required a steam engine and engine house, a hot air oven to provide the blast, plus other support facilities. Though it was considered sophisticated, newer methods of smelting had been developed that used coal instead of charcoal to fire the furnace. However, the Catoctin region had trees, not coal, and so Catoctin Furnace operated the less-efficient Isabella.

Fitzhugh also built a mule-powered rail system to bring ore from the pits to be washed and then dumped in Catoctin Furnace.

The Fitzhugh operation ran deep in debt, so much so that he sold a half interest in the operation to Jacob Kunkel in 1856. For $35,000, Kunkel owned half of 7,000 acres, the iron works, six teams of horses and mules, harnesses, coal on hand, 1,400 cords of wood on hand, the ore mined, furnace, railroad cars, furnace tools, blacksmith and carpenter's tools, furnace tools, wagons, carts, farming utensils and mules. The agreement was that Fitzhugh would operate the furnace for a year and apply the proceeds to the partnership debt, according to Frederick County land records.

Again to War

As America divided and fought its Civil War beginning in 1861, the next legend, and probably the least-defensible one, concerning Catoctin Furnace arose. It was said that the plates for the ironclad *U.S.S. Monitor*, which fought its way into history against the *Merrimac* in 1862, were cast at Catoctin Furnace.

"The claim that Catoctin made iron for the Monitor is based on nothing more solid than a reference to "Frederick Citizen" in a popular history of Frederick County, a reference that is worthless. Until reliable evidence is found, this claim will also have to be abandoned," according to Porter's 1936 federal government report.

That book is the *History of Frederick County* by Thomas J.C. Williams and Folger McKinsey. It was published in

1910 and does not source the footnote.

Other than this, no records exist to refute or verify the claim.

The iron-plated hull of the U.S.S. Monitor. Photo courtesy of the Library of Congress.

"What we do know is the H. Abbott and Sons of Baltimore supplied the rolled plates for the *Monitor*'s gun turret. What we do not know – and are constantly on the lookout for – is with whom they, or in fact any of the firms associated with the *Monitor*, subcontracted. To date we have found nothing conclusive.

"According to information we have here on Catoctin Furnace, it appears that Catoctin primarily produced pig iron –

so it is unlikely that they supplied iron for the turret plates. This is mentioned in William Still's 1987 work, *Monitor Builders*.

"It may be that Catoctin Furnace participated in the building of a monitor-class vessel – just not the *Monitor*. Again – there is no proof either way," Anna Holloway, Chief Curator of The Mariners' Museum in Newport News, Virginia, wrote in an e-mail to the author.

However, Holloway goes on to say it can't be discounted entirely. "What we are finding is that the names, invoices and such from a variety of firms are beginning to reveal themselves through newly discovered archival material relating to the *Monitor*," she wrote.

Building a community

Jacob Kunkel and his brother John ran the furnace until 1866 when Jacob sold his interest to John. John ran it until 1885.

He built "Deborah," a 50-foot high anthracite coal and coke furnace about 140 feet south of Isabella. It was a steam and water powered furnace with a daily capacity of 35 tons of pig iron. With Deborah and Isabella both producing coal, Catoctin Furnace's annual output doubled to 1,200 tons a year.

Deborah, a 50-foot high anthracite coal and coke furnace was built it is believed on the site of the original furnace. Whereas the previous two furnaces had been shorter rectangular structures, Deborah was cylindrical. Annual output was nearly doubled to 1,200 tons a year.

During the Kunkel years, Catoctin Furnace also became a community of grist mills, 80 houses for workers and a company store. The furnace employed 100 workers plus 300 wood-choppers and colliers. It included 11,000 acres. According to

Mentzer, the furnace hands at this time averaged about $3.72 a week because the work was not considered skilled work.

This was also a prosperous time for business. The ore banks were extended to accommodate the additional production.

When John Kunkel died in 1885, his children organized the Catoctin Iron Company. This only lasted until 1887 when the operation closed and went into receivership. The receivers operated the furnace for a year when Catoctin Mountain Iron Company was formed. The operation output 30 tons of pig iron a day and lasted until 1892 when the falling price of iron made it unprofitable.

The Blue Mountain Iron and Steel Company bought the operation in 1899 and began making pig iron the next year. The output was 40 tons a day and lasted until 1903.

Joseph Thropp bought the operation in 1906 for $51,135. He dismantled the ironworks but continued the mining operations. The ore was shipped to his furnaces in Pennsylvania to be smelted.

Lancelot Jacques and a Mr. Hauver bought the property in 1923. He sold the property off in tracts.

President Herbert Hoover's secretary Lawrence Richey bought one in 1929, and the president occasionally camped on the grounds until the land became a federal park during the Great Depression in 1937. The National Park Service turned over 4,500 acres to the Maryland Park System in 1954.

The Furnace Today

Not much remains today of Catoctin Furnace, but what there is can be seen near Cunningham Falls State Park south of Thurmont.

Of the three furnaces, only Isabella remains, but you can walk inside the casting shed and look at where the fires once burned.

The remnants of the ironmaster's mansion sit nearby, though it no longer overlooks the furnace. Some of the stone walls and fireplaces remain to give visitors an idea of how large the house used to be.

You can also walk on a self-guided trail that will take you between slag heaps that are now covered over with dirt and grass.

The remaining stack of the Catoctin Iron Furnace. Photo courtesy of the National Park Service.

Supreme Court Justice Dedicates Memorial Named After a Bird

O n May 23, 1953, about 350 boys and probably just as many adults gathered on the banks of Hunting Creek where the Thurmont Food Bank now sits. The boys were at the end of a three-day campout where they were taught how to fly fish.

The adults included men like U.S. Supreme Court Chief Justice William Douglas; U.S. Senators J. Glenn Beall, John M. Butler and A. Willis Robertson; Congressman DeWitt S. Hyde and former Maryland Governor Preston Lane. They were there to dedicate a memorial to deceased members of the Brotherhood of the Jungle Cock.

While the name of the group sounds like the title to a bad porn movie, Ken Crawford, president of the Jungle Cocks at the time said in the *Frederick Post,* "Our only aim is to teach youngsters the art of fishing. ... We just want to teach them to have more fun while fishing, to observe the rule of the sport, and to take a hand in the conservation of our fish, game and natural resources."

Though the group had been founded in Thurmont in 1939, it had spread to other states.

"The concept of teaching youngsters about fishing and conservation of our natural resources was the ground work for the formation of the Brotherhood," Thomas W. Cooney wrote in his article, "A History of the Brotherhood of the Jungle Cock."

The group's earliest roots can be traced to when Joseph W. Brooks, Jr., J. Hammond Brown and Frank Burt Smoot launched *The Junior Outdoorsman*. The Maryland State Game and Fish Protective Association published the magazine explicitly directed at young boys.

The Brotherhood of the Jungle Cock memorial in Thurmont.

Brooks was the chairman of the Fresh Water Committee of the Maryland State Game and Fish Protective Association, and Brown was president of the association. Another founding member, Frank L. Bentz, Sr., was the public relations director of the Maryland Game and Inland Fish Commission.

Brooks and Brown encouraged Bentz to arrange a weekend outing on Big Hunting Creek. Invitations were mailed on the letterhead of The Maryland State Game and Fish Protective Association to association members and to the Outdoor Writers Association of America, as well as other guests, according to Cooney.

Twenty-five men attended that first outing on the opening day of trout season in 1939. They were so pleased with the event that they decided to continue it annually as "The Anglers Campfire."

However, the next year, a late snow froze the anglers' fishing lines, and so they stayed in their cabins.

"As the men sat in the warmth of the lodge there was talk of fishing and the perpetuation of the sport, the environment, and the conservation of our natural heritage. It was decided that an organization be formed that would address the concerns of the group, and that the focus must be on tomorrow's inheritors," Cooney wrote.

On May 21, 1940, the anglers met again and voted to call their group, "The Brotherhood of the Jungle Cock". The name refers to the male Asiatic Jungle Fowl, whose feathers are highly sought after for fishing flies.

The monument, which was sculpted by William Carter Wescott, showed a man and boy in their fishing gear. The boy is grinning as he displays his trout that he caught on his fly rod. The man is stooping to release the fish from the boy's line. The figures were cast in bronze and set on a 64-inch high base made of stones from Hunting Creek.

Douglas gave the dedicatory address at the ceremony and then presented the memorial to Crawford. Crawford, in turn, then presented the monument to Thurmont Mayor C. Ray Weddle, who accepted it on behalf of the town. The town had also donated the land where the memorial was placed.

The monument still greets visitors who park at the town office.

Red-Hot Iron in Loudoun

W hile Catoctin Furnace at the northern end of the mountain was a long-running business venture beginning in 1774, iron was also smelted along the southern end of the mountain. It was the success of iron smelting at Catoctin Furnace that helped make iron smelting in Loudoun County a reality.

The Johnson Brothers – Thomas, James, Baker, and Roger – dissolved their partnership running Catoctin Furnace in 1793. At that point, Thomas and Baker took over running it. Thomas also began looking for other opportunities. He and at least two of his brothers found it at the southern end of Catoctin Mountain.

During the time, Thomas was the governor of Maryland, he and his brothers, and Josias Clapham formed a new company that purchased 1,310 acres in Loudoun County at $10 an acre. Loudoun historian Eugene Scheel noted in his article, "When Iron Was Hot in Loudoun County" that this was a bargain price, about half the going rate for arable land. This had happened the year before the Johnson brothers dissolved their Catoctin Furnace partnership.

While the Johnsons had notoriety in Maryland and Frederick County, Clapham was their equal in Virginia. He was a General Assembly delegate for 12 years and a director of the Patowmack Canal, which was the forerunner of the Chesapeake and Ohio Canal.

The plan was for the canal to transport iron to the new armory at Harpers Ferry or east to Washington.

Thomas Johnson. Photo courtesy of Wikimedia Commons.

It was an area rich in the raw materials needed to run a furnace.

An 1856 report by G. Jenkins Phillips noted, "The indications of ore are very great upon the surface; large blocks lie promiscuously upon the top of the ground, and nearly everywhere the surface itself would make iron."

The new iron furnace called Potomac Furnace used

hardwoods from Catoctin Mountain to heat the furnaces and water from Catoctin Creek to keep the furnaces from overheating.

When a bridge was constructed at Point of Rocks, the furnace owners began shipping refined ore along the Baltimore and Ohio Railroad.

"James Higgins, the state agricultural chemist of Maryland, estimated 1.2 million tons had been removed from the mine in its 60 years," Scheel wrote.

John W. Geary, a Pennsylvania businessman, and Michael P. Kern, a Baltimore businessman, bought the Potomac Furnace property in 1856 for $100,000. It looked like a sound investment at first, but then the ironmaster, Howard James "a gentleman but with one arm, but that was as good as two arms of some men," according to historian Briscoe Goodhart in the *Loudoun Mirror*, died.

This tragedy was followed by an economic depression that stalled sales in 1857. When Geary found himself deep in debt, he sold his shares in the company to pay off his creditors.

Just as Catoctin Furnace died a slow death, so did the Potomac Furnace, which was now called the Potomac Iron Company. It continued minimal operations until 1870 when the furnace was converted to a lime kiln.

"The Mansion burned, the log huts decayed, and about all that was plainly visible of the furnace tract when I first saw it some 40 years ago were open pits, strewn with iron deposits, on the east side of Route 15 by Awbrey's Spring Branch," Scheel wrote.

Today the site is covered with homes.

At its peak before the Civil War, Loudon County was Virginia's second-largest iron producer.

Thurmont's House of Matches

J acob Weller was a blacksmith and the grandson of one of the founders of Mechanicstown, Md. He knew how to make tools, and he did that well in his shop across the street from his house. He was proud of his work, so proud in fact, that you often see his name as "Jacob Weller, B.S." for Jacob Weller, blacksmith.

Jacob was born on January 25, 1775. He was the oldest of nine children born to Jacob and Anna Krall Weller. Jacob married Anna Margaret Weller in 1800. She was the grand-daughter of another unrelated Weller family that was also one of the founders of Mechanicstown. They had five children before Anna died in 1816. Jacob remarried the following year, and he and Mary Love had 10 children.

Besides being a blacksmith, Jacob also proved himself an entrepreneur. He began investing in real estate in August 1805. His first property purchases in Mechanicstown were two lots on the north side of Main Street. Here he built a large stone house for his family, but it was also used as Mechanicstown's first inn.

"He built the first inn in town, had his blacksmith shop, had his hand in a couple of mills and his family helped found two churches," said Thurmont historian John Kinnaird.

Weller purchased two acres on the south side of Main Street in Mechanicstown across the street from his home. There he built a one and half story stone building with a workshop behind it. In the workshop, Weller operated his edged-tool factory. He made axes, shovels, hoes and other tools using the flowing water of Hunting Creek to cool the metal.

"Weller was a good blacksmith, but he became more famous for developing matches," Kinnaird said.

The Thurmont Match House in 1910 before the second story was added. Photo courtesy of Thurmontimages.com.

Fire On a Stick

Weller was a curious man with interests beyond iron. In the early 1800s, he saw a set of French matches while he was on a trip to Frederick. He marveled at how a wooden stick struck against an abrasive could ignite quicker than flint and steel. What's more, a person using a match didn't have to hope that the spark would catch on kindling. Matches nearly always created a small flame that quickly ignited, and the matchstick itself served as the initial kindling.

Weller recognized the matches' usefulness, and his mind began to work on how he could make his own matches.

"Using his father's library plus his own technical skills, he discovered the secret of the sulphur-tipped sticks and soon began their manufacture," Michael Spaur wrote in the *Frederick Post.*

Though matches are mass produced today, in 1825 when Weller began making them, "Their process was slow and laborious, each splint having to be cut and dipped separately in the composition which formed its head," James Cooke Mills wrote in *Searchlights on Some American Industries.*

The match splints were hand cut from basswood or other softwoods.

"The matches were made from a block of softwood that was cut in a cross-hatch. Then the tips were dipped in his secret recipe. Then you would break off each match individually as you needed one," Kinnaird said.

The match block was a 2-inch cube that contained between 100 and 150 matches, according to Spaur. The matches were packaged in a box along with a small piece of sandpaper and sold for 25 cents a box.

History of Matches

Robert Boyle, an Irish physicist, created the first thing that could be thought of as a match in 1669. He coated a piece of paper with phosphorous and a small portion of wood with sulfur. When he rubbed the paper across the wood, he created a fire.

However, though he had all of the elements, Boyle failed to turn them into a match.

Most accounts list Englishman John Walker as the creator of friction matches in 1827. However, Weller began manufacturing his matches in 1825 after he got the idea from French matches. Weller's matches also more closely resembled what we consider matches today.

Walker made his matches on yard-long sticks and called them "sulphuretted peroxide strikables." He used antimony sulfide, potassium chlorate, gum and starch in his formula. The match stick was dipped in the formula and allowed to dry. It ignited when the stick was struck against a hard surface.

At the same time, Weller's and Walker's friction matches were being developed, some inventors created a Promethean match. Introduced in 1828, a Promethean match had a small glass bulb containing sulfuric acid and coated with potassium chlorate, sugar, and gum and then wrapped in paper. A person bit down on the glass bulb to strike the match. Because it wasn't as easy to use as a friction match, its popularity quickly died out.

A set of Weller's friction matches made at the Match House. Photo courtesy of Thurmontimages.com.

Marketing the Devil's Work

Although Weller's formula for a match head turned out to be a simple one, it was a dangerous one. Experiments with mixing and refining the formula resulted in several explosions in the workshop, local historian Anne Cissel wrote in an article "Jacob Weller: America's first manufacturer of stick matches" in *Thurmont Scrapbook: Glimpses of History*.

Jacob and his son Joseph met with a lot of resistance when trying to sell their matches. People were suspicious of something that could become flammable so easily.

"Peddlers whom Jacob Weller sent out to market his flame-producing bits of wood, often encountered vigorous sales resistance, often expressed by the sharp teeth of the householder's dogs. Many wild tales swept through the countryside. The frontier folk warned each other that these new fire sticks would explode and blow a man, his family and his earthly possessions high into the peaceful Maryland sky," George Wireman wrote in his book *Gateway to the Mountain*.

Weller's early matches were called lucifers, perhaps because their flammable tips came from a red brimstone mixture. Whatever the reason, it would prove not to be the best choice for a name because many people already thought matches were the work of the devil.

"'Instant fire' was not readily accepted by many religious sects," Spaur wrote.

Failure to Patent

Others soon recognized the usefulness of the matches, and by 1832, lucifers were well known in the area. Though Weller was a clever inventor and manufacturer, he didn't patent his version of the match. Enterprising business people purchased Weller's lucifers and used them as patterns to create their own versions. A Massachusetts man secured the first American patent on matches in 1836.

This mistake led Weller to financial ruin in the late 1830's. Weller became an "insolvent debtor" and trustees sold off his properties. He died in 1846 and was buried in the cemetery of the church his family helped establish. At the time, the church was known at Weller's Church, but today, it is Weller's United Methodist Church.

The Match House in the 1970s on West Main Street. Photo courtesy of Thurmontimages.com.

The Match House Today

Today the Match House still stands where it always has in Thurmont, Md. It is a private house owned by John and Susan Laugher, and the workshop is long gone.

"We didn't know about its history when we bought it," said John Laugher. "The previous owners and our neighbor told us about it."

The Laughers haven't made any significant changes to the house, John Laugher said former owners over the years had made changes that made the house ineligible to the on the National Register of Historic Homes.

"The original match house was a single story, but sometime in the past, a second story was added, and there's an addition on the back," Laugher said.

Despite not being formally recognized as historical, Laugher still enjoys living in a home where history was made nearly two centuries ago.

"The Match House is very important to Thurmont's history," Kinnaird said. "Very few small communities have a major first like having the first commercially produced friction matches made there."

A County Called Catoctin

C an you imagine a Catoctin County, Maryland? It would have included Frederick County north of Walkersville, Md., and Mechanicstown, Md., would have been the county seat.

It was a dream that some people in the northern Frederick County area pursued throughout 1871 and 1872. The *Catoctin Clarion* was only on its 10th issue when it carried a lengthy front-page article signed with the pen name Phocion. Phocion had been an Athenian politician, statesman, and strategos in Ancient Greece.

Creating a new county had been talked about within groups of people for a while, and it was time to garner support by taking the issue to a broader, general audience.

"Some sober sided citizens in our valley are quietly discussing the question among themselves, shall Frederick county be divided and the new county of Catoctin be erected into a separate organization?" the newspaper reported. Wicomico County had been formed in 1867 from portions of Somerset and Worcester counties, so the idea of another new Maryland county was not far-fetched. In fact, Garrett County would be formed from the western portion of Allegany County in 1872.

The main reason put forth for creating a new county was the distance and expense of traveling to Frederick, Md., to register deeds and attend court. Opponents argued that creating a new county would be costly for the citizens of the new county. New county buildings would have to be constructed and county positions filled. All of this financial burden would have to be absorbed by the smaller population in the new county.

"Our neighbors across the Monocacy in the Taneytown District have but a short distance to go to attend Carroll county Court. Why shall we on this side be deprived privileges which were granted to them? Shall the people on one side of the Monocacy be granted immunities which are to be withheld from citizens residing on the other side?" the *Clarion* reported.

Besides northern Frederick County, Phocion said that in Carroll County, Md., residents of Middleburg, Pipe Creek, and Sam's Creek were also interested in becoming part of Catoctin County.

"If a majority of the citizens residing in Frederick, Carroll and Washington counties (within the limits of the proposed new county), favor a division, I see no reason why it should not be accomplished," the newspaper reported.

In deciding on what the boundaries of the new county would be, three conditions needed to be met in Maryland. 1) The majority of citizens in the areas that would make up the new county would have to vote to create the county. 2) The population of white inhabitants in the proposed county could not be less than 10,000. 3) The population in the counties losing land could not be less than 10,000 white residents.

Interest reached the point where a public meeting was held on January 6, 1872, at the Mechanicstown Academy "for the purpose of taking the preliminary steps for the formation of a New County out of portions of Frederick, Carroll and Washington counties," the *Clarion* reported.

Dr. William White was appointed the chairman of the committee with Joseph A. Gernand and Isaiah E. Hahn, vice presidents, and Capt. Martin Rouzer and Joseph W. Davidson, secretaries.

By January 1872, the *Clarion* was declaring, "We are as near united up this way on the New County Question as people generally are on any mooted project—New County, Railroad, iron and coal mines, or any other issue of public importance."

Despite this interest in a new county, by February the idea had vanished inexplicably from the newspapers. It wasn't until 10 years later that a few articles made allusions as to what had happened. An 1882 article noted, "It was to this town principally that all looked for the men who would do the hard fighting and stand the brunt of the battle, for to her would come the reward, the court house of the new county. The cause of the sudden cessation of all interest is too well known to require notices and only comment necessary is, that an interest in the *general* good was not, by far, to account for the death of the 'New County' movement. Frederick city, in her *finesse* in that matter, gave herself a record for shrewdness that few players ever achieve."

A letter to the editor the following year said that the men leading the New County Movement had been "bought off, so to speak, by the promises of office, elective at the hand of one party, appointive at the hands of the other, and thus the very backbone taken out of the movement." The letter also noted that the taxes in Frederick County were now higher than they had been when a new county had been talked about and that they wouldn't have been any higher than that in the new county. "And advantages would have been nearer and communication more direct," the letter writer noted.

Catoctin County, Virginia

Nearly 150 years later, Virginians started talking about forming a Catoctin County that would be created from western Loudoun County. The proposed county would include

Loudoun County west of the Catoctin Mountain water-shed. Purcellville, Va., would become the seat of the new Catoctin County.

The movement began in 2005 with a letter to the *Washington Post* and has waxed and waned since then.

The idea took root because residents in the western end of Loudon County wanted to fight the rapid development encroaching in the area. Interest faded but was then reignited when an extension of the D.C. Metro silver line was proposed, resulting in higher taxes for county residents.

The group supporting the new county has even created a website. It points out that the people of western Loudoun County are feeling disenfranchised with their county representation.

"Our representatives on the Board have been forbidden from placing items on the agenda concerning the vital zoning of our land and the Chairman of our County, elected by county-wide vote, has been stripped of his powers. The current Vice Chairman, a representative from one small area of the County, now holds the Chairman's rightful powers. Our homes, our livelihoods and the very quality of the lives we lead in Western Loudoun are all on the line and we have no say in our own future if our destiny is tied to the suburbanized east."

Another problem, according to the website, is that a Virginia Supreme Court ruling has reversed growth controls in the western end of the county, supposedly because of a technicality.

While there is still no Catoctin County, the idea continues to live.

The Railroad vs. the Canal at Point of Rocks

A
t the turn of the century, canals were quite popular in the United States. The country was expanding westward, and those people wanted a way to bring their products to where the bulk of the population was in the east. Canal popularity peaked in 1850, which is also the same year the Chesapeake and Ohio Canal reached Cumberland, Md. There were 4,000 miles of canal in the U.S. with the C&O making up nearly 5 percent of that amount.

Although the National Road was completed in 1818, it was still 30 times more expensive to move goods along the road than by a canal. It was estimated at the time that four horses could pull one-ton by wagon for 12 miles in one day. However, on a canal, those same four horses could pull 100 tons 24 miles in a day.

The Federal government in its infinite wisdom decided to back this still favorite form of transportation while ignoring the new technology called railroad. Construction of the canal began on July 4, 1828, the same day as construction on the Baltimore and Ohio Railroad began. And as the name suggests, both groups were heading to Ohio.

The C&O Canal was America's "Great National Project" of the early 19th Century.

The reason people other than George Washington were interested in building canals was that Americans were pushing west from the coastline. In 1800, 19 percent of the U.S.

population lived west of the Alleghenies. By 1830, it was up to 27 percent of the population. These people needed goods from the east that they couldn't find on the frontier and they needed to be able to ship their products to the eastern cities and seaboard ports.

The question was how to get those items between the two points.

The construction on the National Road from Cumberland to Vandalia, Illinois, started in 1811. It was a slow route, though faster than the mash-up of roads and turnpikes one would have to take otherwise. It was its era's interstate. There were also maintenance problems that plagued it.

After George Washington's Potowmack Company in the early 1800s had failed, it was still believed that a flatwater canal alongside the Potomac River would work.

The C&O Canal was chartered in 1825 to accomplish this.

The C&O Canal was a construction and engineering challenge for its time. The charter required that 100 operable miles be built in five years. Benjamin Wright who had overseen the building of the Erie Canal was chosen for the same job on the C&O.

The canal construction involved more than just digging a trench across level land and making it watertight. Boats traveling from Georgetown to Cumberland had to be lifted more than 600 feet on their westward journey.

The 184.5-mile-long canal was built in sections bid out to independent contractors. The laborers were mainly imported Irishman, who jumped at the chance to come to America, though they quickly found the work unsatisfying. The work was hard, and the tools were picks, shovels, horses and black powder.

Shortages of suitable building materials and money quickly set in slowing the progress. Then there was the escalating cost to purchase land.

When completed, the canal had 11 aqueducts, 74 lift locks, 160 culverts, and 12 river feeder locks and guard locks.

Point of Rocks

The canal was watered by dams built on the Potomac River. As the canal construction reached one of the barriers, water was allowed to flow into the completed portion of the canal. The first dam was at Little Falls. When the canal reached that point, that first section of the canal was placed into operation.

This happened in the summer of 1831.

Point of Rocks during the Civil War. You can see how close the canal, the railroad, and the mountain are at this point.

However, the second dam was at Harpers Ferry and to reach that point, the canal would have to pass through a narrow area of land called Point of Rocks, and that's where the forward progress of the canal stopped.

The B&O Railroad was claiming the right of way through Point of Rocks. Canal officers thought the canal had the rights to by its own charter and the charter of the Potowmack Company which it had taken over. Both the canal and the railroad couldn't pass through the narrow area of usable land between the Potomac River and Catoctin Mountain.

A locomotive passes a canal boat at one of the spots where they two run side by side. Photo courtesy of the National Park Service.

The canal has just assumed its rights were secure while the railroad was aggressively trying to defend its claim including getting waivers from landowners in the area, including Charles Carroll, who was an early supporter of the railroad and one of the wealthiest men in the country.

The case went to court and stayed there four years, during which time the canal could make no progress. Meanwhile, construction on the railroad continued. The case was eventually decided for the canal but left it a financial wreck. The federal government with a new administration had grown disillusioned with the idea of the canal and stopped supporting it. The canal company had to find new funding from the State of Maryland. The railroad had to wait to build through Point of Rocks until after the canal finished its construction.

This meant that the canal and railroad were running side by side through Point of Rocks. This happens in a couple areas along the canal. These areas allowed for some venting of frustration. The train engineers would show their animosity toward the canal by blowing their whistles when they passed canal boats in the hopes of startling the mules.

Once the legal hurdles were cleared, the canal company restarted construction. Once the canal passed through Point of Rocks, the B&O Railroad managed to make their own passage through the area with the aid of tunnels. I could then connect its track on both sides of Catoctin Mountain.

Although the C&O Canal won the legal battle at Point of Rocks, by the time it reached Cumberland, the railroad had already been there eight years securing its trade position.

There's Gold in That There Hill!

━━━━━━━━━━━━━━━━━━━━━━━━━━━━━━━━━━━━━

I n 1936, Harry Baumgartner stood before groups of investors and held up small vials of gold dust and nuggets. It caught the attention of the crowd as he told them that the gold had come from beneath Frederick County soil in the foothills of Catoctin Mountain. *The Baltimore Sun* described the site as being "Five miles west of Frederick, in a wooded dell among the first round foothills of the Blue Ridge…"

In 1933, Baumgartner had been prospecting in Virginia when he realized the soil composition that he suspected was hiding gold was similar to the soil found in Frederick County, his hometown. So his refocused his attention to the county.

In November 1934, he sent a sample to Baltimore to be assayed. The chemists and assayers tested the ore and reported that it showed .22 ounces of gold per ton. With gold trading at $35 per ounce (about $620 per ounce in today's dollars), this meant that there was about $7.70 (about $136 in today's dollars) in gold per ton of raw material.

This excited Baumgartner. Since the sample was from close to the surface, he expected that the amount of gold would increase with deeper mining. Also, the sample he had sent to Baltimore had also shown .38 ounces of silver per ton that could also be mined.

While most people associate gold with mines in the western states, this was not the first time that gold had been discovered in Maryland. Gold was first found in the state in the early 1800s, but it wasn't commercially mined until after the

Civil War, according to GoldRushNuggets.com.

"The majority of the gold that has been recovered here is found in the northern and central parts of the state. Unlike much of the gold on the east coast which are limited to glacial deposits, there are actually lode gold deposits present here, with several dozen mines that have been worked since the original discovery of gold," according to the website.

The state's peak production was about a decade in the future, and it was only 1,000 ounces of gold. Besides Frederick, gold in Maryland was found in the Catonsville area, the Liberty area, the Simpsonville area, the Woodbine area, and the Great Falls area.

Baumgardner secured the mineral rights for 70 acres from George and Joe Cramer for 10 percent of the gold mined from the site. Baumgardner also hired Arthur King, Gorman King, and Charles Carpenter to start digging at 25 cents an hour. Robert Cartwright, a mining engineer from Los Angeles, was hired to oversee the operation.

"Except for the pits and trenches dug in the hillside, mounds of stone thrown up by the diggers, scattered odds and ends of machinery and an unpainted wooden shanty erected as a tool shed, the place looks like any other peaceful, pretty little mountain vale," *The Sun* reported.

With gold in one hand and report in the other, Baumgardner began searching for investors.

"When the organization first began, everyone was afraid to put any money into it. No one believed that there was any gold in Braddock, or in Frederick County for that matter," Mary Baugher, wife of miner Roy Baugher, told the *Frederick Post* in 1979.

This was also the height of the Great Depression, so money was hard to come by for many people, and the prospects for the mine just didn't seem promising. According to

The Sun, up until this time only $71,684 had been mined in Maryland and most of that had been done before 1906.

Baumgardner must have been persuasive, though, because people started to buy stock in the company, which was called the Clifton Gold Mine. *The Sun* also noted that "Barely a day passes that some stock salesman, speculator or mining engineer doesn't turn off the National Highway at Clifton to the diggings."

He eventually raised between $25,000 and $30,000 in capital, and he went to work improving the operation. He built a testing lab, improved the machinery, sunk a 137-foot shaft and hired nine men to dig.

By 1939, reports were that the mine was showing three ounces of gold per ton, which was worth $108, according to the *Frederick Post*. It was not enough to support the operation, which by this time was running two 10-hour shifts of 12 men each.

Baumgardner got more bad news in 1939. A report showed that while there was gold in the ground, it was at least 200 feet deeper than the mine was at the time.

He soon declared bankruptcy, the mine was closed, and the equipment was auctioned off. Some of the miners expressed their doubt that there had ever been any gold mined at the site. They told the *Frederick Post* in 1979 that they had never seen any gold.

Donald Cartwright, the son of the mining engineer, disagreed. "There is gold in the Baumgardner mine. They really just never had a chance to get off the ground; never had enough money," he told the newspaper.

A Road By Any Other Name

U.S. Route 15 runs roughly parallel to the east side of Catoctin Mountain, allowing a traveler to go from the northern end of the mountain to the southern end in about an hour. The highway is much longer than the mountain, though. The 792-mile-long highway runs from runs from Walterboro, S. C., to Painted Post, N. Y. It passes through South Carolina, North Carolina, Virginia, Maryland, Pennsylvania, and New York.

The highway is also known by a number of different names depending on where you are on the road: Journey Through Hallowed Ground, James Monroe Highway, Catoctin Mountain Scenic Byway, Jefferson National Pike, Frederick Freeway, and 115th Regiment Memorial Highway are all names for Route 15 as it runs beside Catoctin Mountain.

However, the highway is predated by an even older road with an entirely different name. Route 15 was once known as the Carolina Road. Although it was only a dirt road about 10 feet wide, it was the major north-south road in the area.

"The road was favored by Colonists – as it had been favored by their predecessors, the Algonquin and Iroquois Indians – because of numerous springs along its route, milder temperatures east of the mountains and relatively safe fords across major rivers and streams," historian Eugene Scheel wrote in his article "The Carolina Road."

Although the Carolina Road does not follow Route 15's entirety, they are both roughly the same from Frederick to Leesburg.

Maryland historian Thomas Scarf estimated that the Carolina Road began in 1740, running from Frederick to Occaneechie Island in the Roanoke River.

"The goods sent from Frederick were boots and shoes, saddles and harness, woolen goods, linen and woolen and flax seed threads. They were carried on pack horses and were exchanged [in Virginia and North Carolina] for cotton, indigo, and money," Scharf wrote.

One of the historical road markers
along the Old Carolina Road.

The road began even earlier than Scharf says, though. Harrison Williams wrote in his book *Legends of Loudoun* that the road started as a game trail used by animals, which were then followed by Native American hunters. He wrote that the Carolina Road "owes its origin to a beaten trail made by the heavier animals of the forest, it was probably used by the Manahoacks and their predecessor tribes long before the Susquehannocks frequented it in the latter half of the seventeenth century, not only on their trading journeys between the Dutch of Manhattan and the Carolina Indians, but in their war forays as well."

Native Americans also used the road to not only travel but to fight. Burials mounds located near the road attest to the fact that significant numbers of Native Americans died nearby. One story in Loudoun County tells of the Catawba and Lenape Indians fighting near the road just south of present-day Leesburg, according to Williams. He wrote, "The surviving conquerors gathered together the bodies of their slain tribesmen and over them toiled to erect the mounds that still stand. The mounds and many hundred acres of surrounding land were early acquired by the Mead family, who later built nearby Greenway, and in that family the legend was handed down that in the springtime of each year, about the anniversary of the battle, there came through the forest a band of Indians who, when they reached the mounds, conducted weird mourning rites for their fallen brethren, made offerings of arrows and food and then disappeared in the surrounding woods as silently as they came."

Just as Route 15 would be known by different names, so was the Carolina Road. It was sometimes called the Shenandoah Hunting Path due to its use by Native Americans, but its use by a less reputable group earned it the name the Rogues Road. It is a name that can be found in land grants in Loudoun County from the mid-1700s.

Because of the road's popularity among horse and cattle thieves, the Virginia Assembly passed a law in 1742 that required people driving stock along the colony's public highways to have a bill of sale available that could be shown to any justice of the peace who might ask to see it.

Besides thieves, highwaymen also traveled the road coming robberies against others. A famous highwayman of the day was named Captain Harper, who like Robin Hood, was said to rob the rich and aid the poor. It was said that travelers and people who lived near the road lived in fear of Captain Harper and his men robbing them, and women would not travel the road alone.

Harry T. Harrison wrote in the 1916 *Loudoun Times*, "A rather pretty story is related in this connection—a young Virginia maiden was walking this road alone one evening about twilight, hurrying from a visit to a neighbour, when a dashing cavalier rode up and reined his horse beside her. 'Are you not afraid to walk this road alone on account of Captain Harper and his band?' he asked. 'No' replied the maiden 'for I have always heard Captain Harper was a gentleman.' The dashing horseman looked at her a moment and then walked his horse beside her until she reached the gate leading to her home. And then raising his hat and bowing he said: 'Captain Harper bids you good night' and digging the rowels into his steed he vanished as he came."

Even then, the story is more legend than fact. Little, if any, evidence exists of highwaymen along the road, especially the Robin Hood-like Captain Harper.

The Carolina Road's value as a route of travel can be seen in the Civil War when Fort Beauregard was established at Leesburg, in part, to protect the Carolina Road and Alexandria and Winchester Turnpike approaches to the town.

When America began building its highways for automobile travel in the early 20th century, the old Carolina Road was incorporated into U.S. Route 15 to become one of the nation's earliest highways, opening in 1926.

The original U.S. Route 15 did not enter Maryland. What is currently Route 15 from Frederick, Md., to Harrisburg, Pa., was called U.S. 240 at the time. In 1927, U.S. 240 became the primary route between Washington, D.C., and Frederick, and Route 15 was extended from Leesburg north into Maryland through Point of Rocks, Md., and connected with U.S. 240 in Frederick, and U.S. 240 from Frederick north became U.S. Route 15.

Call it what you will. U.S. Route 15 is still a beautiful highway to travel to see natural beauty and historic sites.

Acknowledgments

I wanted to thank all of those people who helped me put the *Secrets of Catoctin Mountain* together. The longer I work as a writer, the more I realize that while one person may publish a book, the effort is much richer when others assist.

To that end, I'd like to thank John Kinnaird and Mary Mannix. They were generous with their time when I had questions, and John also allowed me to use some of his pictures in this book, and they also were available to answer questions I might have throughout the process. Mary, in particular, is a wealth of knowledge in the Frederick County Public Library's Maryland Room.

I'd also like to thank Deb Spalding, publisher of *The Catoctin Banner*; Guy Fletcher, editor of *Frederick Magazine;* Holly Smith, former editor of *Maryland Life*; and Ray Buchheister, former publisher of The Dispatch Community Newspapers. All of them have been willing to publish my history articles over the years.

Finally, I'd like to thank Grace Eyler for not only another great-looking cover but also being able to create the template for the Secrets series.

I have probably missed someone who I'll remember after this book goes to print. If so, it's not because I didn't appreciate your input. I sometimes get confused juggling all of the projects that I do. If I did leave you out, mention it to me.

In putting together *Secrets of Catoctin Mountain*, I found it interesting, how events and people between the northern, central, and southern areas of Catoctin Mountain paralleled or overlapped each other from creating a new county to hunting a monster.

It made me realize that I was right in including the entire mountain in the stories I covered. There are probably lots more that I'll discover now that this book is out. Never fear! I can always write a *Secrets of Catoctin Mountain II.*

James Rada, Jr.
January 30, 2017

About the Author

J ames Rada, Jr. has written many works of historical fiction and non-fiction history. They include the popular books *Saving Shallmar: Christmas Spirit in a Coal Town, Canawlers,* and *Battlefield Angels: The Daughters of Charity Work as Civil War Nurses.*

He lives in Gettysburg, Pa., where he works as a free-lance writer. James has received numerous awards from the Maryland-Delaware-DC Press Association, Associated Press, Maryland State Teachers Association, Society of Profession-al Journalists, and Community Newspapers Holdings, Inc. for his newspaper writing.

If you would like to be kept up to date on new books be-ing published by James or ask him questions, he can be reached by e-mail at *jimrada@yahoo.com.*

To see James' other books or to order copies online, go to *www.jamesrada.com.*

PLEASE LEAVE A REVIEW
If you enjoyed this book, please help other readers find it. Reviews help the author get more exposure for his books. Please take a few minutes to review this book at *Amazon.com* **or** *Goodreads.com.* **Thank you, and if you sign up for my mailing list at** *jamesrada.com***, you can get FREE ebooks.**

Don't Miss These Books By James Rada, Jr.

Secrets of Garrett County: Little-Known Stories & Hidden History from Maryland's Westernmost County

Known for its natural beauty, Garrett County is made up of interesting people, places, and events that make it unique. From the time the CIA poisoned people with LSD at Deep Creek Lake to the story of the Black Widow Murderess of Grantsville, these stories will intrigue you. *Secrets of Garrett County* includes 44 fascinating stories and 58 pictures.

The Last to Fall: The 1922 March, Battles, & Deaths of U.S. Marines at Gettysburg

In 1922, a quarter of the U.S. Marine Corps marched from Quantico, Va., to Gettysburg, Pa., where they conducted historical re-enactments of Pickett's Charge for 100,000 spectators. The Marines also conducted modern versions of the battle with tanks, machine guns, and airplanes. Two Marines were killed on the battlefield during the exercises making them the last military line-of-duty deaths on the Gettysburg Battlefield.

Available wherever books are sold.

Made in the
USA
Middletown, DE